# Wild Places of Mid Wales

## A Guide to Protected Wildlife Sites

compiled by

Andrew Jenkinson

for

# Contents

|  | Page no. |
|---|---|
| Map of Nature Reserves | iii |
| Foreword by David Bellamy | iv |
| Introduction | v |
| Useful Addresses | x |
| Using this Guide | xii |

## Site Descriptions:

| | Site no. | | Site no. |
|---|---|---|---|
| Morfa Harlech | 1 | Cors Caron | 21 |
| Coed Crafnant | 2 | Dinas | 22 |
| Coed Ganllwyd | 3 | Vicarage Meadows | 23 |
| Mawddach Valley | 4 | Nant Irfon | 24 |
| Cregennan | 5 | Elan Valley | 25 |
| Aber Corris | 6 | Dyffryn Wood | 26 |
| Ynys-hir | 7 | Gilfach Farm | 27 |
| Ynyslas | 8 | Bailey Einon | 28 |
| Glaslyn | 9 | Burfa Bog | 29 |
| Coed Gwernafon | 10 | Withybeds & Wentes Meadow | 30 |
| Llyn Mawr | 11 | Fron Wood / Garth Dingle | 31 |
| Lake Vyrnwy | 12 | Llandeilo Graban | 32 |
| Coed Pendugwm | 13 | Pwllpatti | 33 |
| Cwm y Wydden | 14 | Brechfa Pool | 34 |
| Llanymynech Rocks | 15 | Park Wood | 35 |
| Gaer Fawr Wood | 16 | Pwll-y-Wrach | 36 |
| Llyn Coed y Dinas | 17 | Daudraeth Illtud | 37 |
| Dolydd Hafren | 18 | Craig Cerrig-gleisiad | 38 |
| Roundton Hill | 19 | Craig y Cilau | 39 |
| Coed Rheidol | 20 | Welsh Wildlife Centre | 40 |

# The Protected Wild Places of Mid Wales

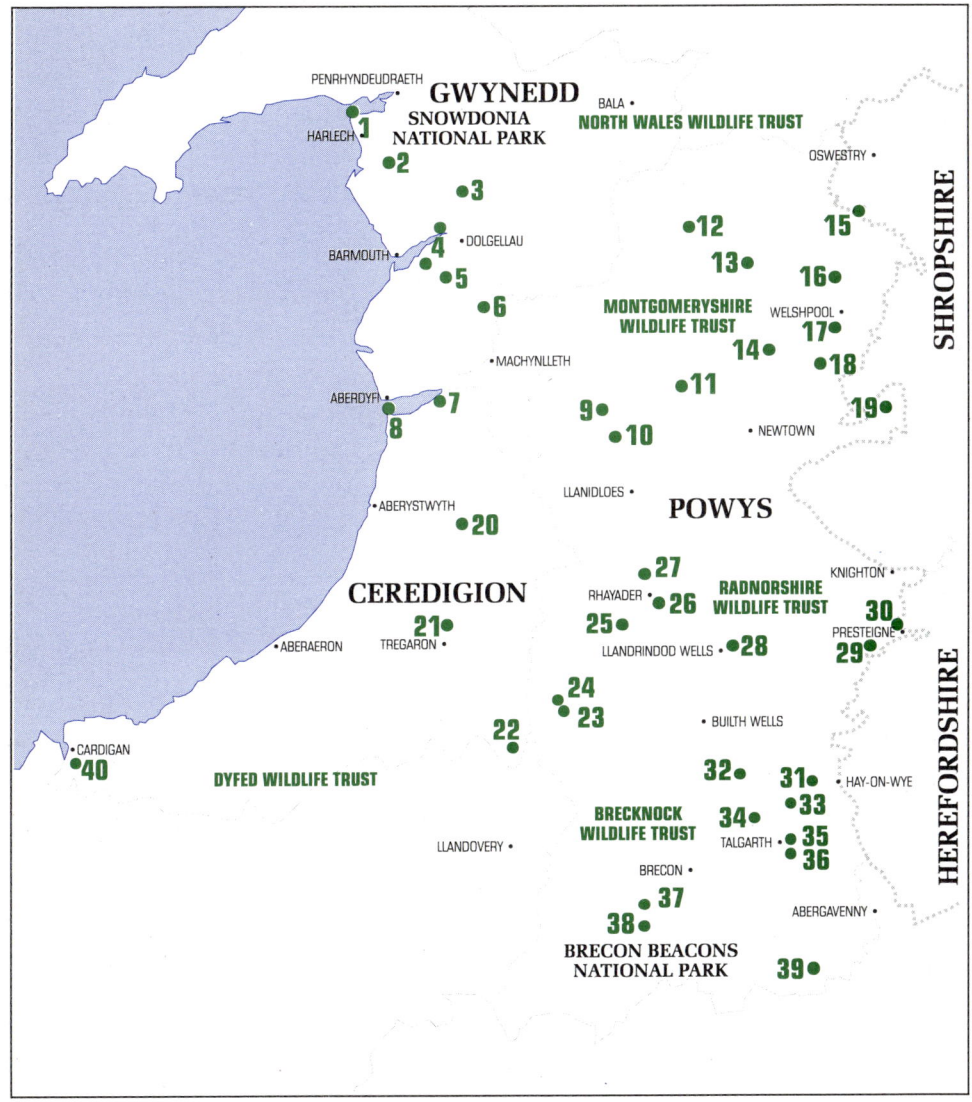

The geographical responsibilities of the Wildlife Trusts are based on counties, or groups of counties, prior to local government reorganisation in 1974. The local authorities currently responsible for providing local services and information are those created in 1996.

The coverage loosely defined as Mid Wales is that adopted by the Festival of the Countryside using local authority boundaries that existed up to 1996. It more or less coincides with the current counties of Powys, Ceredigion and the southern (previously Meirionnydd) part of Gwynedd.

# Foreword

I keep returning to Mid Wales. The countryside and scenery are magnificent and each visit is a breath of fresh air and constant delight. How pleasing then to be asked as President of the Wildlife Trusts, and Chairman of the Festival of the Countryside, to be asked to write a short introduction for this welcome new guide.

This book is a collection of some of the best places in Mid Wales to see wildlife. The locations featured are "wild" in the truest sense as they are nature reserves owned or managed by wildlife trusts and other conservation organisations. These reserves play an immensely important part in helping to conserve wild plants and animals. But reserves also have another important part to play – letting people see, learn and understand more about the wildlife they contain.

I'm convinced that knowledge is the key to effective conservation. The more we know and understand about wildlife around us the better we'll be able to look after it. Use this book to guide you to some of the best wildlife watching sites in Mid Wales. This book is meant to be used. Use the impressive amount of information responsibly and wisely and you can be sure that your visits to the wild places of Mid Wales will all be hugely enjoyable.

I wish you well on your travels in this magical part of Britain.

David Bellamy

# Introduction

## What is a Wild Place?

The image that brings many visitors to Mid Wales is one of rugged grandeur and wilderness. Surely it must be full of "wild places", not a mere 40 or so described in the following pages?

In part that is true, but this book admits to a hidden agenda with its own definition of "wild places" as those which are owned and managed by conservation organisations specifically for the benefit of their wild animals and plants. These are the places where wildlife is guaranteed and afforded protection as the primary land use of the site. They are also the places where those responsible for wildlife conservation want you to be able to see and enjoy the wildlife without undue restriction on access.

Virtually none of Mid Wales is strictly wild in the primaeval sense. That is, it does not look now as it would if humans had not interfered with it over the millennia. The process of woodland clearance began with the first farmers almost 5000 years ago. Since then the countryside has been part-and-parcel of the natural human environment. It has been the source of fuel and food. Trees have been cut down and replanted; domesticated animals have grazed from the highest hill tops to the river valleys; minerals have been exploited.

Until quite recent time – about the last 50 years with the universal arrival of the tractor – all this human activity was limited in practical ways by the natural constraints of soils, slopes and climate. And that was a significant restriction in a part of the country where the hard and ancient rocks give rise to high land with predominantly acid soils and the moist south westerly winds sweep in a rainfall generally above 125cm a year.

But as the internal combustion engine replaced the horse, many of these constraints applied no longer. Steeper slopes could be ploughed; wetter soils could be drained; higher pasture could be re-seeded and fed with chemical fertilisers to yield worthwhile crops.

In the woods the demand was no longer for the small poles of coppiced oak or hazel, or for hardwood pit props, or bark for tanning. Wood was needed in ever increasing quantities but of a sort that would grow fast and straight in a poor climate.

The Welsh hills took on new hues – the bright grass green of nitrate enriched pasture and sombre green of coniferous plantations. Wildlife could no longer survive in the same way in natural harmony with agriculture and forestry. We cannot stop, let alone put back, the clock of progress. It is inherent in the nature of human beings that we strive to be more efficient in the production of our food and to raise our material standard of living, though there may not be universal acceptance of the yardsticks used to measure efficiency or wealth. So active nature conservation has been forced upon us.

A number of people, concerned at the possible demise of the wild animals and plants that were such a feature of our countryside, began to take positive steps towards environmental conservation. A new influence on countryside management was born.

The result is that we have a separate land use classification of "nature reserve". It is that classification which forms the basis of the wild places described here. Nature conservation is not quite the same as landscape conservation. In the two National Parks that fall at least in part into Mid Wales – Snowdonia in the north and Brecon Beacons in the south – as well as in the areas that enjoy the lesser protection of being designated Areas of Outstanding Natural Beauty, you will find plenty of places that appear wild, or in some cases just bleak, depending on your taste. And that is the crucial point. Landscape beauty, like any other, is in the eye of the beholder.

You will find plenty of wildlife in the mountains, over the moors, in the woods and spinneys and along the hedgebanks of country lanes; but its tenure is insecure. It is dependent on the continuation of traditional methods of management. That is what protection within nature reserves hopes to achieve. Much of what we cherish and admire is the result of particular forms of land management. There would be no "natural" hay meadows with their riot of summer flowers and attendant butterflies, little open moorland with its haunting call of the curlew, few accessible woods with glades and clearings, if the land had not been managed and created that way over the centuries.

There is a lot more to nature conservation than simply putting a ring fence around a cherished plot. Many hours have to be spent by volunteers (usually) removing scrub growth from grassland, coppicing woods to let in more light or arranging for sheep and cattle to continue their traditional role of keeping grass short in meadow and pastures.

## Who protects Wild Places?

In the forefront of this positive and proactive conservation movement are the Wildlife Trusts. There are now 48 such Trusts covering each English and Welsh county, and a number of urban wildlife groups. They are linked as The Wildlife Trusts under the umbrella of the Royal

Society for Nature Conservation. Their main aim and role is to be a local grass roots conservation organisation, holding and managing nature reserves for the purposes of both species and habitat conservation. At the same time they have a powerful educational role both directly with schools and at more informal levels through providing help and advice to a large range of organisations on wildlife conservation issues.

It is the nature reserves of the five Wildlife Trusts whose territory between them covers Mid Wales that form the majority of entries in this guide. Nationally the Trusts work closely with the Countryside Council for Wales (CCW) – the official advisory body on nature conservation. CCW is responsible amongst other things for designating National Nature Reserves. These are sites of national importance, selected by CCW to protect the best examples of different habitats and the animals and plants that depend on them. Several of these, where the habitat is very fragile, the species very rare or access for the public is dangerous, are not included in the guide. But equally several are included where provision can be made for safe public access and enjoyment, giving everyone the opportunity to visit these very special sites. Some are already enjoyed recreationally by thousands of visitors every year, such as the sand dunes at Ynyslas. Others, such as Nant Irfon, derive much of their atmosphere from the rugged landscape and relative wilderness, but are freely available to all who enjoy such spots.

Some aspects of nature have enjoyed protection for a long time. The Royal Society for the Protection of Birds evolved from the "anti-plumage" Society for the Protection of Birds established in 1889. With a royal charter in 1904 it soon broadened its remit beyond the plumage trade and set out to protect wild birds in all ways possible. Its most conspicuous successes in more recent years have been the establishment of a series of nature reserves, five of which feature in this book, and the protection of individual species. In Mid Wales this work is seen clearly in the remarkable success of the red kite story. You will be unlucky if you don't now have at least one sighting of these magnificent birds of prey during your visit to the region.

Of similar vintage to the RSPB, and now into its second century, is the National Trust. In many people's minds the National Trust is primarily a protector of country houses and other parts of our built heritage; but this is a false image. The Trust began in 1895 to secure threatened countryside, especially in areas like the Lake District, and its very first property was here in Mid Wales – Dinas Oleu, a small patch of open land above Barmouth. Today its holdings are extensive, but included in the guide are just two in Mid Wales where nature conservation is a major factor in Trust ownership and management.

A sprightly newcomer on the conservation land management scene is The Woodland Trust, started in 1975. Like the National Trust, they do not see their role as specifically one of nature conservation. Public access and enjoyment of woods is a major consideration in acquisition and management. But inevitably some of the most attractive woods are also very rich in wildlife. Protection through sympathetic management by the Woodland Trust will perpetuate the conservation value of these woods, and for that reason five of the most accessible and interesting examples are included here.

Several organisations who own and manage land primarily for other purposes also have a remit to take account of nature conservation. Most conspicuous amongst these are the water companies and Forest Enterprise. All have suffered a bad press in the past, imposed largely by the narrowness with which their roles were interpreted. The deep valleys and high rainfall of Mid Wales caused the water companies of 19th century England to look in this direction when seeking supplies for the rapidly expanding towns of Birmingham and Liverpool. The reservoirs of the Elan Valley and Lake Vyrnwy were the result. Reservoirs have proved more of a draw with the general public than the nature conservationist; but now with a positive duty to take account of wildlife on their water catchments, Dwr Cymru Welsh Water at Elan and Severn Trent Water at Vyrnwy are actively involved in managing "wild places".

Relatively cheap land capable of supporting imported conifers was the attraction to the Forestry Commission, set up in 1919 and charged then with the task of establishing a strategic reserve of timber. Planting of huge areas of Mid Wales with blankets of exotic conifers continued apace until the 1970s. New plantations are now less common, and as forests come up for felling the opportunity is taken to replant in ways more sympathetic to landscape and wildlife. There are more broadleaved trees being planted, especially along the edges of forest rides and down valleys. Rides are wider and mown for wildflowers which attract butterflies. Forest Enterprise, the land management arm of the Forestry Commission, is a major provider of recreational opportunities in the countryside. So while we have not listed any of their woods as nature reserves, you will find frequent reference to Forest Enterprise walks and picnic areas in the "Nearby Sites" sections.

In recent years the local authorities – county and district councils – have played an increasingly important role in the protection of wild places. Their planning departments often work closely with the Wildlife Trusts in identifying and restricting development of important wildlife areas. In some cases (for example Withybeds) the local council has leased or given land to a Wildlife Trust to be managed as a nature reserve. At Llandeilo Graban the roadside verges are managed as a nature reserve in agreement with the county council highways department. As you travel around Mid Wales you will find a number of countryside facilities and picnic sites maintained for your enjoyment by the local authorities. And not least they are responsible for the public rights of way network which gives access to all these wonderful "wild places".

Local government reorganisation over the past 25 years may have left you uncertain as to which county you are in. The map on page iv shows the boundaries of the three councils – Powys, Ceredigion and Gwynedd – which, as unitary authorities since April 1996, are responsible for all services in their respective areas.

Thus is made up the rather complex pattern of management and concern for the protected wild places of Mid Wales. But the important thing is that people do care. There are plenty of opportunities for you to go out and enjoy our splendid countryside described in the following pages. The addresses overleaf will provide the main contacts you may need for further information.

# Useful Addresses

**FESTIVAL OF THE COUNTRYSIDE**,
Frolic House, 23 Frolic St, Newtown, Powys SY16 1AP. *Tel: 01686 625384*

The Festival is a partnership initiative in the development and promotion of green tourism in rural Wales. Established in 1985, it has gained an international reputation as a model approach to sustainable rural tourism. The year-round programme consists of over 1000 events, attractions and activities which convey the natural beauty and sense of place of rural Wales, whilst supporting its regional economy.

The programme is published in Festival of the Countryside magazines which are available from Tourist Information Centres and by post from the above address.

## The Wildlife Trusts

Five county Wildlife Trusts manage nature reserves in the area covered by this guide. Between them they have over 80 reserves, of which those mentioned here are only the most accessible or the most interesting to the casual visitor. For further information on the Wildlife Trusts contact the appropriate trust at the address given below.

**BRECKNOCK WILDLIFE TRUST**,
1st Floor Office, 2 The Struet, Brecon, Powys LD3 7LH.
*Tel/fax 01874 625708*

**DYFED WILDLIFE TRUST**,
7 Market Street, Haverfordwest, Pembrokeshire SA61 1NF.
*Tel: 01437 765462; fax: 01437 767163*

**MONTGOMERYSHIRE WILDLIFE TRUST**,
Collot House, 20 Severn Street, Welshpool, Powys SY21 7AD.
*Tel: 01938 555654; fax: 01938 556161*

**NORTH WALES WILDLIFE TRUST**,
367 High Street, Bangor, Gwynedd LL57 1YE.
*Tel: 01248 351541*

**RADNORSHIRE WILDLIFE TRUST**,
Warwick House, High Street, Llandrindod Wells, Powys LD1 6AG.
*Tel/fax: 01597 823298*

## Other Reserve Managers

Nature reserves are also looked after by several other environmental conservation organisations. Those featured in this guide are:

**COUNTRYSIDE COUNCIL FOR WALES,**
Plas Penrhos, Ffordd Penrhos, Bangor, Gwynedd LL57 2LQ.
*Tel: 01248 370444; fax: 01248 370698*

**THE NATIONAL TRUST,**
North Wales Office, Trinity Square, Llandudno, Gwynedd LL30 2DE.
*Tel: 01492 860123; fax: 01492 860223*

**ROYAL SOCIETY FOR THE PROTECTION OF BIRDS,**
Bryn Aderyn, The Bank, Newtown, Powys SY16 2AB.
*Tel: 01686 626678; fax: 01686 626794*

**DŴR CYMRU WELSH WATER,**
Elan Valley Visitor Centre, Rhayader, Powys LD6 5HP.
*Tel: 01597 810898*

**THE WOODLAND TRUST,**
Autumn Park, Grantham, Lincs. NG31 6LL.
*Tel: 01476 581111; fax: 01746 590808*

**FOREST ENTERPRISE,**
Victoria House, Victoria Terrace, Aberystwyth, Ceredigion SY23 2DQ.
*Tel: 01970 612367*

**SEVERN TRENT WATER,**
Shelton, Shrewsbury, Shropshire SY3 8BJ.
*Tel: 01743 265000*

## National Parks

Parts of two National Parks fall within the Mid Wales area. They do not themselves own and manage nature reserves, but do provide information about the wildlife and natural landscapes of the parks.

**BRECON BEACONS NATIONAL PARK AUTHORITY,**
7 Glamorgan Street, Brecon, Powys LD3 7DP.
*Tel: 01874 624437; fax: 01874 622574*

**SNOWDONIA NATIONAL PARK AUTHORITY,**
Penrhyndeudraeth, Gwynedd LL48 6LF.
*Tel: 01766 770274; fax: 01766 771211*

# Using this Guide

The emphasis, as David Bellamy expressed in his foreword, is on using the guide in the field so that you can experience the wealth of wildlife on the reserves at first hand.

We decided on a standard format for each entry. Undoubtedly this obscures some of the differences between sites. Some readers – and site managers – may argue that large, diverse reserves with lots of rarities deserve more space than small patches of woodland or meadow. But generally the big reserves already have much more available information: a reserve leaflet, sign posts, a visitor centre even. Once there, you will not really need the book. Smaller sites may not even have a reserve sign up. We want you to use the book to find those places, and to help you to discover what you might see there.

The nature reserves described here have been arranged as an extended and rather tortuous trail from north to south, thereby grouping sites that are in the same geographical area. Each is given a number for reference to the map on page on iii. The name of the reserve is that used by the managers. This is not always a name that will appear on other maps. The name of the managing authority does not necessarily imply ownership. Sometimes sites are looked after by conservation agencies under lease or management agreements. But if you want further information then contact the site manager at the address given on pages x-xi. Each managing body is distinguished by the symbol shown beside the address, but in some cases this is a modification of the official logo of that organisation.

### How to get there:

The location map, of variable scale but always orientated with north at the top, should help you locate the position of a reserve sufficiently to know where to look for it. For those reserves that are off main roads you are strongly advised to refer to the appropriate Landranger (LR) Ordnance Survey map at a scale of 1:50,000 (approx. 1¼ inches to the mile) or the more detailed Pathfinder (PF) map at a scale of 1:25,000 (2½ inches to the mile). In some areas of the National Parks the Pathfinder Maps are combined into special Leisure Maps (LM) which contain more visitor information and cover a larger area per sheet. Sheet numbers for these maps are given below each location map, along with the National Grid Reference. Instructions for using grid references are given on each Ordnance Survey map.

Access is described in terms of availability of the site to the public, sometimes with a comment on the difficulty or otherwise of walking.

Parking arrangements are briefly described, but please note that at many sites there is no formal car park. It is then necessary to use a convenient lay-by or roadside parking area. Always ensure that you are not obstructing either the highway or access to fields or houses. On single track lanes never park in designated passing places.

We would like to think that, as a contribution to environmental improvement, you will visit reserves by public transport. In practice that is often an unrealistic hope. We have indicated what public transport is available, but for full details of times and routes consult the local Tourist Information Centre. Postbuses reach some surprisingly remote spots twice a day, giving the chance to get out to say Abergwesyn, explore a reserve and return in the afternoon.

It is notoriously difficult to say how long a visit will take. Your interest, the weather, time of year and many other factors play a part. But we have indicated our view of how long a worthwhile visit might take in the hope that you can plan your days out accordingly.

## What to See

Though the longest section of each entry, the description of what to see was also the most difficult to write. Wildlife rarely performs on cue! Many birds are migratory, mammals nocturnal and plants briefly flowering. Turn up at the wrong time in poor weather and a reserve might offer little compared with what you will see at a different season. Although the author has visited at least part of each reserve at some time, the accounts are based largely on details supplied by the site managers. They too err on the side of caution, but also have a tendency to under-estimate the interest of the ordinary at the expense of the rarity. Indeed, official species lists often do not mention the existence of the common species at all! Most sites are therefore described mainly in terms of the type of habitat you will find. Special features of the reserves are mentioned where they are significant and likely to be seen (at the right time of year of course); and aspects of management are frequently underlined.

It is important to remember that nature reserves, like other parts of the landscape, support only that wildlife which is adapted to live in that habitat. The difference is that on nature reserves wildlife comes first. Go forth and enjoy it – and if you do see something special please let the site owners know. A few pages are provided at the back of the book for you to jot down your own observations.

# 1 ~ Morfa Harlech
## Countryside Council for Wales

*This National Nature Reserve covering over 2,200 acres of dune and estuary is one of the fastest growing sand dune systems in Europe. It shows dunes in all stages of development.*

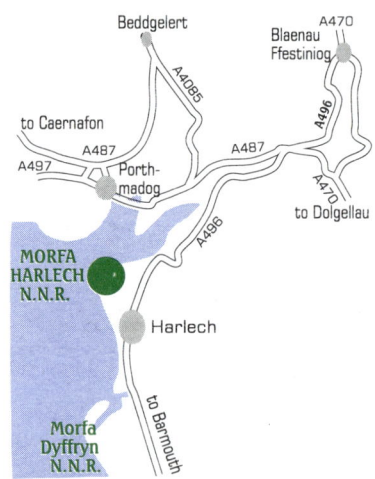

**Maps:** LR 124; Leisure Map 18; Morfa Harlech grid ref: SH 560350.
**Access:** Open only along footpaths to the beach and along the foreshore. Permit required for other parts of the reserves.

**Parking:** Public car park down lane to west off A496 north of Harlech.

**Public Transport:** Train to Harlech station; buses to Harlech (service 38) every few hours on A496.

**Contact:** CCW Regional Office on 01284 370444.

**Facilities:** Leaflet.

**Time:** You will need a whole day to explore the entire area.

## How to get there

Easily found along the main coast road, the A496. Turn off to the car park just north of Harlech and the railway crossing.

## What to see

At first sight this might appear to be uninteresting as a National Nature Reserve – little but rolling sand dunes covered in marram grass. But it is a genuinely wild place, created by and changing with the forces of nature, not of humans. The dunes here are actively growing with a constant supply of sand being blown inland from the north of Barmouth Bay. The sand accumulates there, having been deposited by the rivers that had washed it down from the mountains of Snowdonia. The land here is rising, not only from accumulation of sand, but because the north west of Britain is gradually rising. When Harlech castle was built in 1274 it was right on the sea shore!

Dunes grow first with sand building up around some obstruction such as seaweed or debris on the shore. Once the embryo dune starts growing, specially adapted plants like marram grass can take hold. This grass is deep

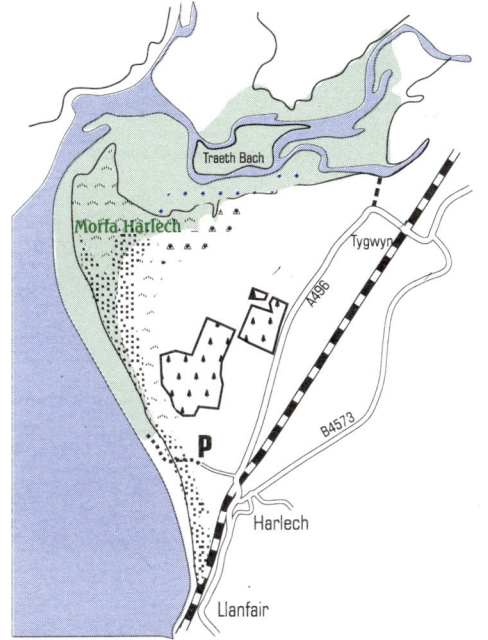

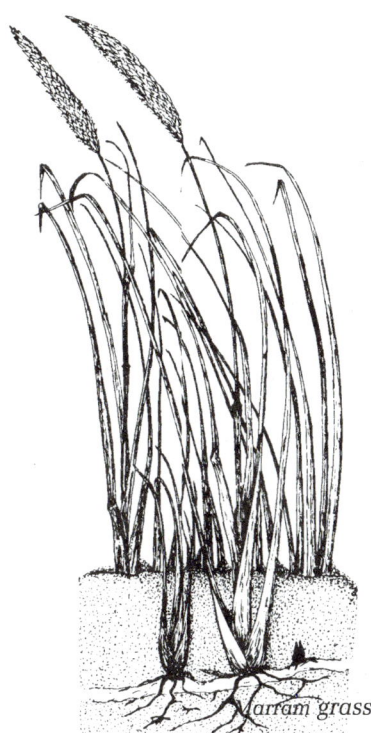

*Marram grass*

rooted and can grow rapidly to keep pace with sand that might smother it.

Further inland the dunes become more vegetated. Other grasses and a variety of plants adapted to the special conditions of very dry soil and salty atmosphere grow on them.

Morfa Harlech is also a good place for birdwatching, especially in winter when you might see whooper swans and large flocks of wigeon and mallard. Hundreds of curlew and oystercatcher also congregate on the mudflats to the north.

## Nearby Sites

Morfa Harlech is just the northern end of a sand dune system that stretches right down to the Mawddach estuary. Other parts of this are conserved for their wildlife interest; notably Morfa Dyffryn to the south of Harlech which is also a National Nature Reserve and the small area at Harlech owned by the National Trust called Maes Llandanwg.

North of the A487 the Vale of Ffestiniog is flanked by large areas of broadleaved woodland, many parts of which are either National Nature Reserves (like Coed Maentwrog) or owned by conservation bodies such as the National Trust's Coed Cai Fali. The narrow gauge Ffestiniog Railway gives good views of these woods.

For a panoramic overview of the area, visit Harlech Castle and look down from the walls on what was clearly sea in the not too distant past.

# 2 ~ Coed Crafnant
## North Wales Wildlife Trust

*This 122 acre reserve is a splendid introduction to the ancient sessile oak woodland of Wales. The tree canopy preserves the humid conditions beloved of mosses, liverworts, lichens and ferns.*

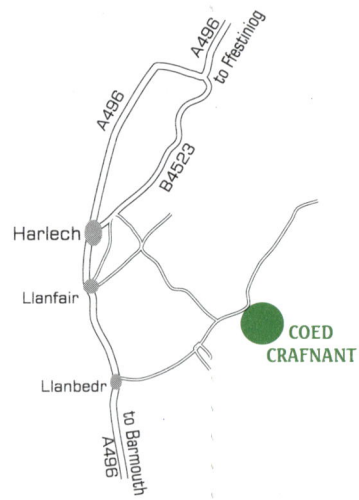

**Maps:** LR 124; PF Leisure map 18; grid ref: SH 619289.

**Access:** Open at all times off public footpath, but no proper paths through the reserve. Keep to line shown on map. It is recommended that you always visit this reserve with someone else.

**Parking:** Limited, but roadside parking for up to 3 cars at grid ref. 617290. Very restricted parking up rough track at southern end.

**Public Transport:** None.

**Contact:** NWWT on 01248 351541.

**Facilities:** Leaflet.

**Time:** This reserve is worth two or three hours for a reasonable exploration.

## How to get there

Turn east off the A496 in Llanbedr on the road to Cwm Bychan. Follow this lane as it winds up the Artro valley for about 4½km. Pass the small hamlet of Pen-y-bont and on to where a track clearly leads down to the river crossing. Park on the roadside (NOT down the track), walk down, over the river, past the old barn, cross the stile and up the track until you see the reserve gate ahead as the path bears away left uphill. Turning off down the rough gated track at Pen-y-bont leads to a very small parking area at the south.

## What to see

The reserve climbs steeply up over the benches formed from resistant bands of grits. Amongst these strata are some manganese-rich beds which provide more alkaline soils, reflected in plants such as woodruff and ramsons. But most of the wood is neutral to acid, particularly so where the soil is thin and the vegetation heathy. In the ill drained area beneath the "vantage point", cotton grass, bog asphodel, bog pimpernel and sundew are found.

But the real joy of this reserve is its atmosphere – literally. You sense the

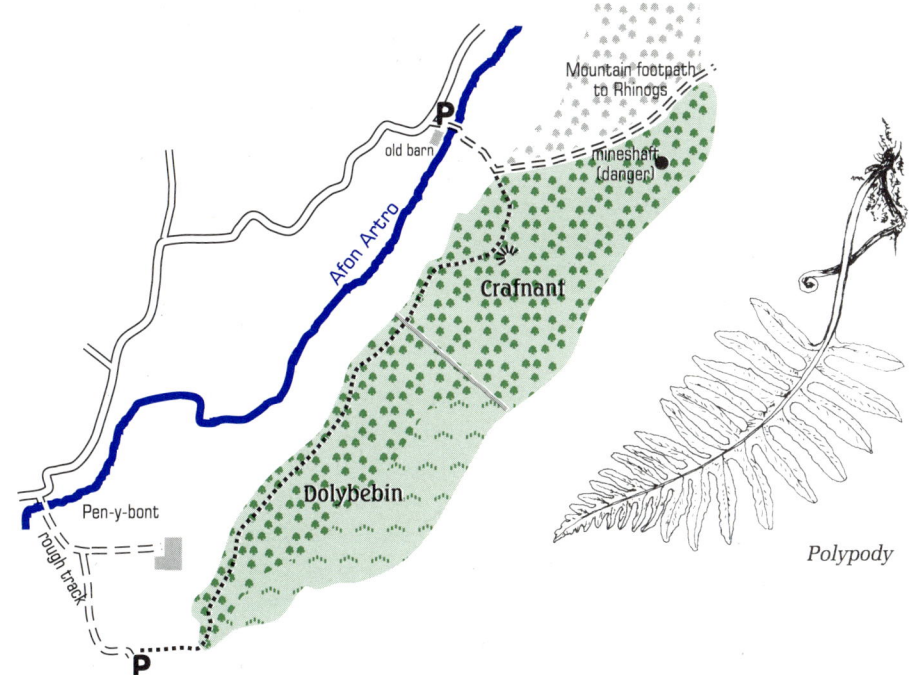

*Polypody*

antiquity of the ancient oaks at the northern (Crafnant) end particularly, growing through a carpet of moss. The trunks and branches are nowhere brown bark, but encrusted in the greys and greens of lichens, mosses, liverworts and the epiphytic ferns (those growing on other plants) such as polypody.

The southern (Dolybebin) part of the reserve is more open, as its trees were felled in 1904 and more oak removed twenty years later. It is now growing up well since the wood was bought as a reserve in 1972 and fenced against the expanding population of feral goats.

## Nearby Sites

Continue up the lane to Cwm Bychan and there is a car park serving the wild and rugged Rhinog National Nature Reserve. From the car park you approach the reserve up the steep path known as the Roman Steps. Tackle this only in good weather and when properly equipped. You can also reach the Rhinog NNR by continuing up the footpath that takes you to the Coed Crafnant reserve. The heather covered upland here is so special it has been declared a Biogenetic Reserve – part of a European network of habitats established to preserve genetic variety amongst the wildlife of Europe.

For a less energetic excursion sample the farm trail or the nature trail on the banks of the Afon Cwmnantcol, the tributary of the Artro which you passed on the way up the lane. Or wander the paths laid out in the Woodland Trust woods of Coed Aber Artro (grid ref. SH 597267) and Coed Lletywalter (grid ref. SH 600275), which are divided only by the lane.

# 3 ~ Coed Ganllwyd
## The National Trust

*A National Nature Reserve on part of the National Trust's Dolmelynllyn estate, this ancient woodland extends up the hill and valley side above the famous Rhaeadr Ddu (Black Falls).*

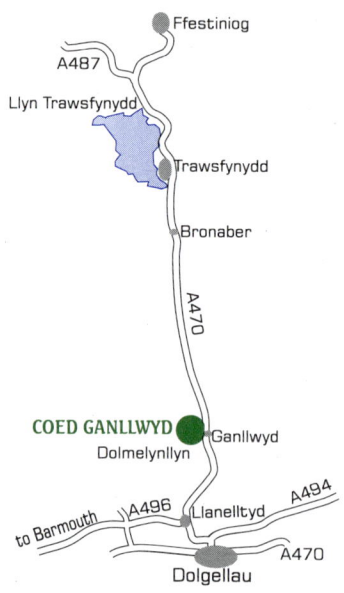

**Maps:** LR 124; Leisure Map 23; grid ref: SH 715245.

**Access:** Open during daylight hours along waymarked routes.

**Parking:** In the small roadside car park on the A470 in Ganllwyd village.

**Public Transport:** Bus every few hours on services 35 and 2.

**Contact:** National Trust Regional Office on 01492 860123.

**Facilities:** Leaflet, waymarked routes.

**Time:** This is a place to visit for at least half a day, possibly more, to see all the estate has to offer.

### How to get there

The Dolmelynllyn estate is easily found on the A470 about 5 miles north from Dolgellau. To explore the estate, which includes the Coed Ganllwyd National Nature Reserve as well as an old gold mine on the moorland of Cefn Coch and ornamental parkland around the house, follow the signposted and waymarked walks across the road from the car park in Ganllwyd village.

### What to see

The main attraction for many are the spectacular Black Falls or Rhaeadr Ddu on the Afon Gamlan. The wet climate that feeds the falls also provides the moist conditions in the gorge to make this the richest site for mosses and liverworts in north west Europe. The rocks and tree trunks are festooned with the green and grey growths of these lowly plants.

The trees largely escaped the fellings through two world wars and survive as an excellent example of the ancient oak woodland of this part of Wales. But it was used and managed woodland nonetheless, with the large trees once being favoured for ship and house

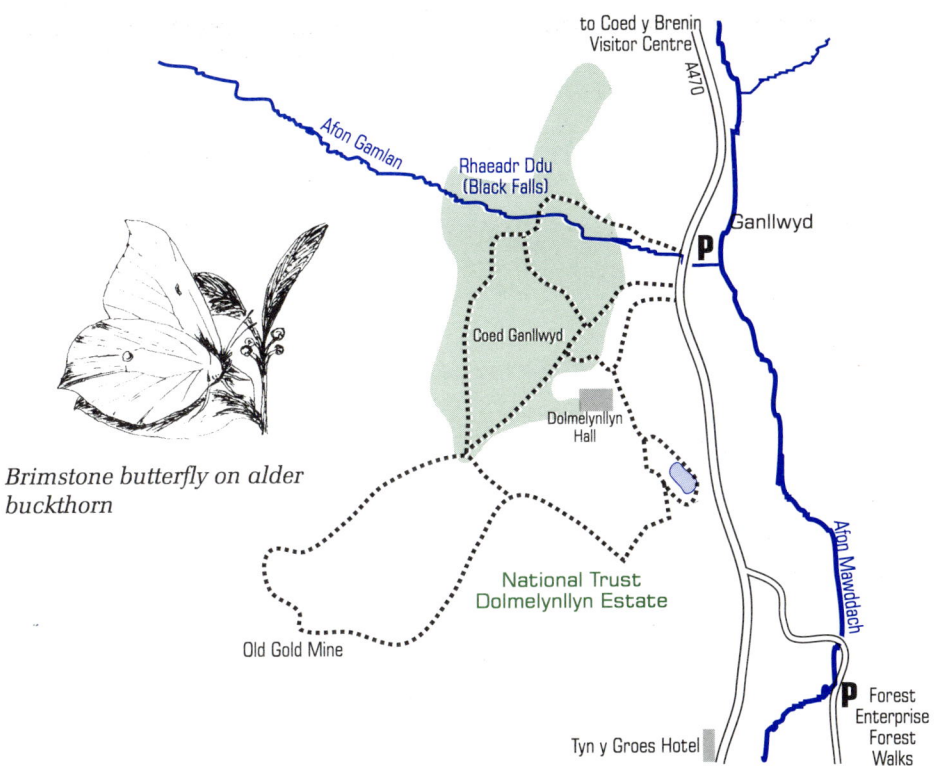

*Brimstone butterfly on alder buckthorn*

building, while the smaller coppiced poles found a multitude of agricultural uses or were burnt for charcoal. Oak bark was harvested for tanning on a large scale.

These old trees and their descendants are home each summer to that most distinctive of Welsh woodland migrants, the pied flycatcher and a host of other woodland birds. This reflects a plentiful food supply, particularly of insects, though jays are partial to acorns. The uncommon brimstone butterfly is found on the Dolmelynllyn estate in association with its food plant, the alder buckthorn.

## Nearby Sites

Take the opportunity of walking all around the Dolmelynllyn estate on the waymarked routes but do not stray from them.

Two miles further up the A470 brings you to the Forest Enterprise Coed y Brenin Visitor Centre. This makes an interesting comparison and contrast with Coed Ganllwyd – the continuation of functional forestry but with very different trees producing a completely different (and generally less favourable) environment for wildlife. There are marked Forest Trails through the extensive plantations both sides of the main road.

# 4 ~ Mawddach Valley

## Royal Society for the Protection of Birds

*This composite site takes in two very different habitats around the Mawddach estuary which are open to the public – the woodland of Coed Garth Gell and the wetland of Arthog Bog.*

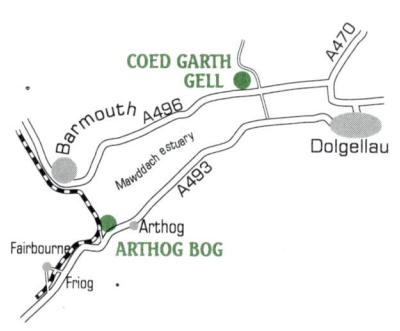

**Maps:** LR 124; Leisure Map 23; grid ref: Coed Garth Gell SH 687195 Arthog Bog SH 632138.

**Access:** Both areas open at all times from public footpaths.

**Parking:** Coed Garth Gell – on roadside lay-by off A496 by Borthwnog Hall Hotel.
Arthog Bog – Morfa Mawddach station.

**Public Transport:** Coed Garth Gell - bus services 38 and 94.
Arthog Bog - Bus 28, 94a, 514
Train to Morfa Mawddach station.

**Contact:** RSPB Wales Office on 01686 626678.

**Facilities:** Visitor centre during summer months at Penmaenpool.

**Time:** You will find plenty to do for a whole day around the Mawddach estuary.

## How to get there

Coed Garth Gell is reached by a short walk from the A496 Barmouth to Dollgellau road, up a footpath that starts opposite the Borthwnog Hall Hotel. Parking is in the lay-by just to the west. Over the toll bridge at Penmaenpool and west down the A493 towards Tywyn and Aberystwyth will bring you to Arthog Bog. Follow the station signs and park at Morfa Mawddach station – or better still arrive by train on the Cambrian Coast line.

## What to see

Coed Garth Gell is a good example of a sessile oak and birch wood, once the main habitat of the hillsides in this part of Wales. Its rich flora of mosses, liverworts and lichens make it a good wood for insects and hence the birds that feed on them – pied flycatcher, redstart, wood warbler and tree pipit.

Largest insects include the pearl bordered and dark green fritillary butterflies.

The 114 acres of wood hangs on the steep valley side and runs right down to the Afon Cwm-mynach where dipper and grey wagtail breed.

Wetland is to the fore in the 12 acres of Arthog Bog, visited in the summer by whitethroat, sedge and grasshopper warblers. Redpolls nest and feed on the alder "cones". In the winter the Bog is visited by the very secretive water rail. The wetter part of the bog has greater spearwort, marsh cinquefoil and the refreshingly fragrant bog myrtle amongst its less common plants.

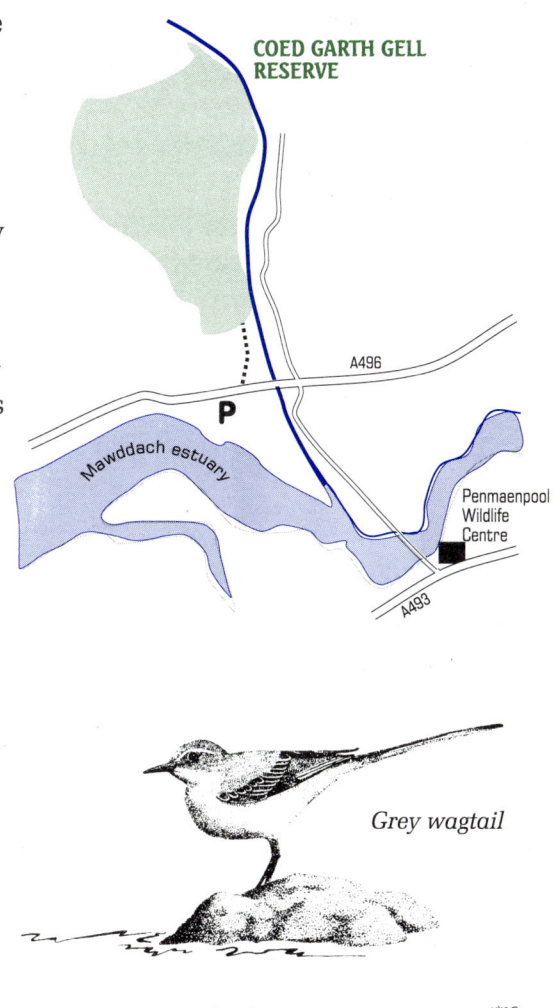

*Grey wagtail*

## Nearby Sites

During the summer months the Penmaenpool Wildlife Centre, run by the RSPB, is open without charge. It is built into the old railway signal box. There is a walk down the trackbed of the old line all the way to Morfa Mawddach – about 4½ miles for the more energetic. There are splendid views out over the estuary, which it skirts for much of its route, ideal for watching waders and wildfowl. This track has been extended eastwards from Penmaenpool for about ¼ mile as a well surfaced path suitable for wheelchairs, with disabled parking, toilets and special picnic tables provided.

Across Barmouth Bridge from Arthog Bog (you can walk over for a small toll) on the hill above the town is Dinas Oleu, the first property purchased by the embryo National Trust in 1896. Around the hillside overlooking the estuary you can enjoy the famous Panorama Walk.

# 5 ~ Cregennan/Cader Idris
## The National Trust / CCW

*The lower slopes to the north of Cader Idris contain the beautiful Cregennan Lakes owned by the National Trust. Above these and over the summit the craggy moorland is a National Nature Reserve.*

**Maps:** LR 124; Leisure Map 23; grid ref: SH 664142.

**Access:** Open on footpaths at all times.

**Parking:** Car park by lakes.

**Public Transport:** Bus 1.5km away in Arthog village.

**Contact:** National Trust Regional Office on 01492 860123.

**Facilities:** Toilets at car park.

**Time**: A short walk in the vicinity of the lakes may only take you half an hour, but allow a full day for an expedition onto the main bulk of Cader Idris.

## How to get there

The recommended approach to Cregennan Lakes is via the road from Dolgellau. This will take you past the Snowdonia National Park car park at Ystradllyn where there is a small exhibition. The direct approach south off the A493 in Arthog is very steep and narrow. For a climb up Cader Idris start at Ystradllyn; or for the south side park at Minffordd on the A487 (GR 732116).

## What to see

This is wild upland country, steeped in myth and legend. While the romantically inclined attribute its features to the work of giants, geologists come up with more prosaic but nonetheless interesting explanations that span hundreds of millions of years. The origin of the rock is volcanic, some of the lavas being poured out under the sea and shaped into bulbous "pillows" that give it the name pillow lava. These are interspersed with layers of ash and other sediments that settled out on the sea bed of the time.

The glaciers of the last ice age scoured and scraped at this hard upfolded rock leaving visible scratches on some of the surfaces and hollowing

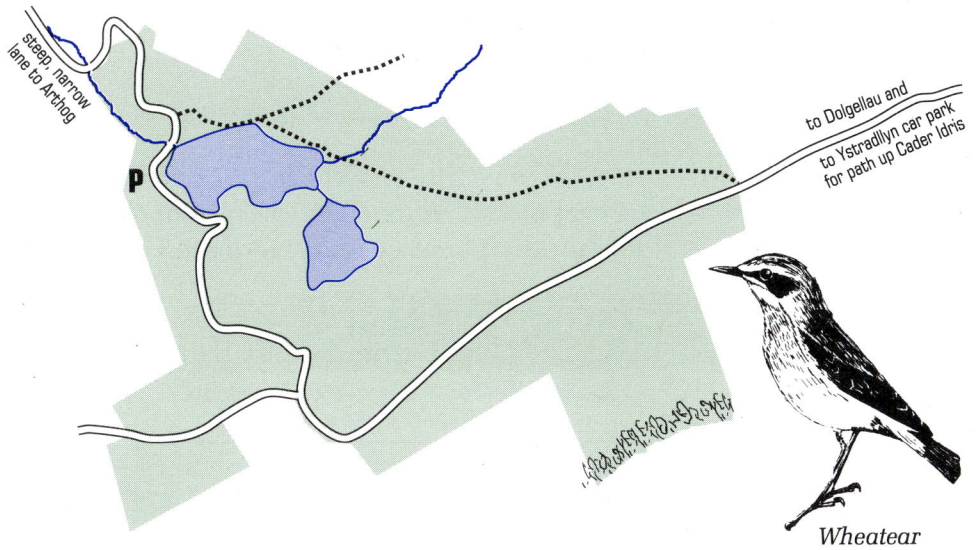

Wheatear

out basins now filled with small lakes such as those at Cregennan on the first "step" up the mountain, or the supposedly bottomless Llyn Cau on the south side.

Amongst this craggy country on the mountain tops there survive rare arctic/alpine flowers, a legacy of the last Ice Age such as purple saxifrage and least willow (a "tree" that never gets to more than a scrambling shrub).

At the lower level around Cregennan the National Trust owns two small hill farms where the rough grazing can be managed in the traditional way. A sign of summer here is the arrival of that dainty visitor, the wheatear, often difficult to spot until it displays its white rump in flight.

## Nearby Sites

When the weather is too bad to venture upwards there is plenty of opportunity to explore the coast. Visit the Mawddach estuary reserves on the previous page.

You can visit a sea cliff inland at Bird Rock in the Dysynni valley (grid ref. 643067) where cormorants come to nest.

For a scenic view of the countryside at a leisurely pace take a trip on the Talyllyn steam railway from Tywyn. You will spot a lot of wildlife from the carriage window; and there are forest walks to follow when you reach the top of the line at Abergynolwyn.

# 6 ~ Aber Corris
## North Wales Wildlife Trust

*These three acres of remnant broadleaved woodland on the steep east bank of the Afon Deri combines the typical woodland habitat with that of the fast-flowing mountain stream below.*

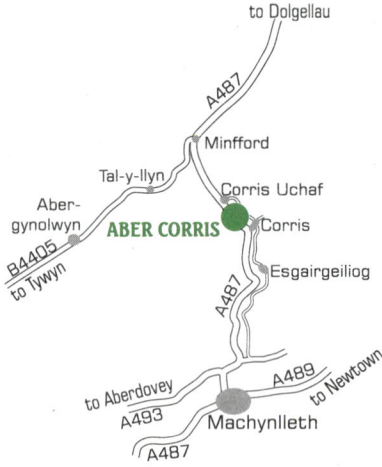

**Maps:** LR 124; Leisure Map 23; grid ref: SH 749085.

**Access:** Open at all times from the public footpath that runs through it.

**Parking:** Pull-in off the A487 about 1 mile south of Corris Uchaf.

**Public Transport:** Bus services 2 and 34 every few hours.

**Contact:** NWWT on 01248 351541.

**Facilities:** None.

**Time:** The accessible area of the reserve by the footpath is only a few minutes walk from the car park. A reserve to pause at for ½ hour when you are passing.

## How to get there

The reserve is easily found just across the river from the A487, half way between Corris and Corris Uchaf. Park in the layby on the east side of the road and take the public footpath over the river.

## What to see

This is one of very few areas of ancient broadleaved woodland left in the Corris valley. Though originally it would have been predominantly oak with birch, and alder in the wetter parts, it has become invaded by sycamore. A major management task is the control of sycamore, as left to itself this is more successful at regenerating than the preferred native oaks.

Other unwelcome colonists that tend to shade out the more interesting plants are bracken, rhododendron and Japanese knotweed. The last two are exotics, rhododendron being widely planted in the 18th and 19th centuries but now running wild, whilst the knotweed was a 19th century introduction from the Far East which grows excessively in damp woodland.

The river is a spawning ground for salmon.

*Sycamore*

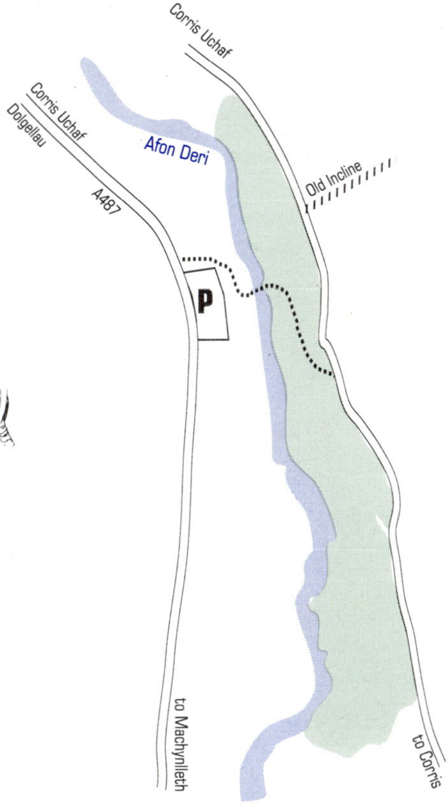

## Nearby Sites

There are plenty of scenically wild places to explore in the vicinity. From Corris village a lane follows the Afon Dulas up into the Dyfi Forest. On the way there are forest trails near Aberllefenni.

Two miles north of the reserve is the start of the south easterly approach to Cader Idris which takes you up past Llyn Cau. For those who don't fancy the climb, turn south westwards down the B4405 alongside Tal-y-llyn Lake. This lake fills a hollow on the flat glacially eroded valley floor – a valley whose straight direction is a result of following a major fault line in the earth's crust.

About three miles south of the reserve on the A487 is a tourist attraction of appeal to all those who are environmentally concerned – the Centre for Alternative Technology.

# 7 ~ Ynys-hir
## Royal Society for the Protection of Birds

*A large and magnificently situated 981 acre reserve on the southern side of the Dyfi estuary, embracing the marsh and both deciduous and conifer woods as the land rises to the rocky hillside.*

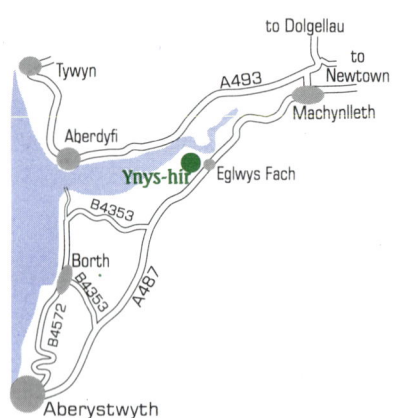

**Maps:** LR 135; PF 905; grid ref: SN 686956.

**Access:** Open daily 9am-9pm or sunset when earlier. (Shop 9-5 except Fridays Nov-March). Charge to non-members of RSPB.

**Parking:** On the reserve at entrance.

**Public Transport:** Bus between Machynlleth and Aberystwyth on A487 (1mile). Railway, Dyfi Junction station 3 miles.

**Contact:** RSPB, 01654 781265.

**Facilities:** Toilets, information centre and small shop. Nature trail around site and observation hides. Guide leaflet.

**Time:** Allow at least 2 hours, more if you wish to explore all the trails.

## How to get there

The approach lane to the reserve is well signed off the A487 Machynlleth to Aberystwyth road on the south edge of Eglwys Fach village. Follow the lane with care as it runs between stone walls dripping with fern, mosses and navelwort. Car parking is just inside the reserve entrance.

## What to see

As always at RSPB reserves the birds put on a splendid show, thanks to the excellent reserve management. Bird watching starts in the car park with a host of birds at the different sections of the bird feeding station (bird table would be a quite inadequate description!). Finches, tits, woodpeckers and nuthatch can all take their fill – and in winter will almost clear out the feeder in the time it takes you to walk round the reserve. Grey squirrels inevitably get a meal out of it as well!

The range of habitats ensures variety and the trails provide a delightful walk even if you come during summer afternoons when birds are least in evidence. The oakwoods support all the characteristic birds of broadleaved woodland including pied flycatcher, redstart, wood warbler and both great and lesser spotted woodpeckers. The too often despised conifers are preferred by goldcrests and coal tits and in winter attract crossbills.

On the river look out for red-breasted merganser, a fish-eating duck with a toothed beak to ensure its catch does not escape. Common sandpiper frequent the river margins. In winter a small flock of Greenland white-fronted geese visit the marsh. They can be seen from the observation hides.

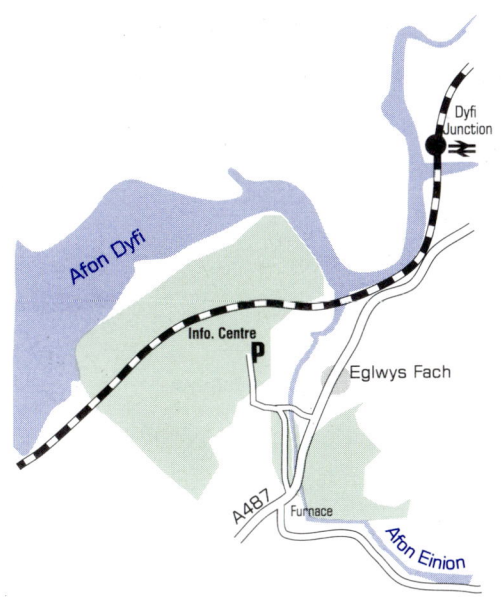

*Crossbill*

## Nearby Sites

There are forest walks and picnic areas in the Forest Enterprise woods up Cwm Einion, turning south off the A487 at Furnace, where both the name and an old watermill proclaim its industrial past.

There is almost no access to the shores of the Dyfi estuary until you reach the mouth at Ynyslas (next page). The broad strip of flat pasture and saltings is all part of the Dyfi National Nature Reserve but access to this area is by permit only. The best, if rather fleeting, view is from the railway train.

# 8 ~ Ynyslas Dunes
## Countryside Council for Wales

*You may not have realised that so popular a recreational beach could also be a National Nature Reserve, of great importance in protecting the distinctive plants and animals of sand dunes.*

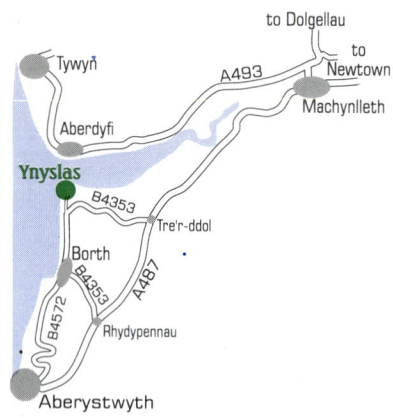

**Maps:** LR 135; PF 905; grid ref: SN 610940

**Access:** Open at all times via the beach road. Information centre open Easter-Mid September, 09.30-17.00.

**Parking:** On the edge of the beach at the end of the road from Borth.

**Public Transport:** Bus 512 Railway station at Borth, 2½ miles.

**Contact:** CCW on 01970 871640.

**Facilities:** Information centre, guides to many aspects of the reserve and to the board walk trail through the dunes; toilets.

**Time:** You will easily spend a whole day here, though the trail through the dunes can be walked in an hour.

## How to get there

Take the B4353 off the A487; at Tre'r-ddol if coming from the north or at Rhydypennau and through Borth from the south. Turn off north up the beach road at Ynyslas and keep on to the end where there is beach parking.

## What to see

Ynyslas Dunes is the seaward part of the much larger Dyfi Estuary National Nature Reserve. This embraces the entire estuary up to high water mark on both sides as far upstream as Dyfi Junction. It also includes the salt marsh on the southern shore and the raised mire known as Cors Fochno or Borth Bog which you can look across to from the top of the dunes. The dunes are the only part of the reserve with easy public access.

Sand dunes, large hillocks of loose blown sand, have built up through a combination of tidal drift northwards along the shore from Borth, material being washed in from seawards at the mouth of the estuary and the flow of sediment coming the other way down the river. The northwards advance of the spit is limited by the outflowing fresh water from the Dyfi estuary.

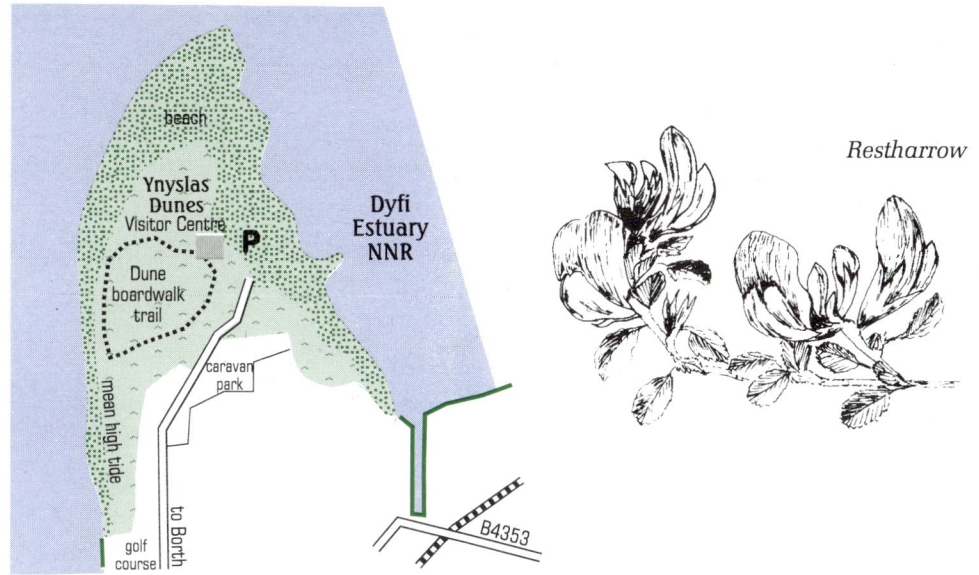

*Restharrow*

The loose sand becomes stabilised by the growth of marram grass in particular. However, if the marram grass cover, or later development of turf is eroded by too much trampling then the whole dune can easily blow away. To protect this fragile environment the path over the dunes is on boardwalks with information panels at intervals. You must keep to the board walks and not walk across the unprotected dunes.

Sand dune plants have to withstand very dry soil conditions and be tolerant of salt. A distinctive group of flowers are therefore found on the dunes. At the highest tide line you may find saltwort with its fleshy green leaves and stems for water storage. Sea rocket is a member of the cabbage family, again with thick fleshy leaves, but conspicuous lilac pink flowers. Apart from the marram grass the unstable dunes may be colonised also by sea spurge, rather like the annual sun spurge garden weed but perennial and tougher, or by restharrow. This member of the pea family has creeping woody stems and pink flowers. On sand dunes it tends to be spiny while on limestone soils inland it lacks the spines.

Ynyslas is of course also a splendid reserve for other life of the sandy sea shore, all described in the visitor centre displays.

## Nearby Sites

The Ynys-hir RSPB reserve (see previous page) lies adjacent to the Dyfi Estuary NNR up towards Dyfi Junction. There is no free public access to Borth Bog.

For a different type of sea shore go to the rocky outcrops and cliffs at the south end of Borth beach.

# 9 ~ Glaslyn
## Montgomeryshire Wildlife Trust

*High on the Plynlimon uplands this large reserve (535 acres) has some of the finest heather moorland in Wales, a lake, blanket bog, a deep ravine and extensive scree slopes and crags.*

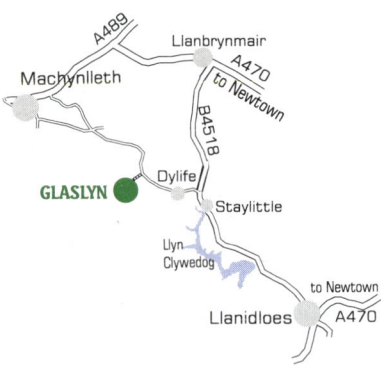

**Maps:** LR 136; PF 907; grid ref: SN 828942.

**Access:** Open at all times. Take extreme care in poor weather. Keep out of the ravine.

**Parking:** At the entrance to the reserve down track off metalled road.

**Public Transport:** None.

**Contact:** MWT on 01938 555654.

**Facilities:** Leaflet to reserve, information panels and walk around lake.

**Time:** It will take you at least a couple of hours to get the full flavour of this site.

## How to get there

This reserve is truly out in the wilds, but can be reached from several directions depending on your starting point. It is approached down a track, south off the minor road that runs steeply over the hills between the B4518 (Llanidloes to Llanbrynmair) and the A489 north of Machynlleth. Go down the track for about a mile off the minor road and park at the reserve entrance.

## What to see

By nature reserve standards this is a really extensive tract of countryside. It embraces many different habitats and is of size sufficient to have a significant impact on the local wildlife, providing a worthwhile territory for birds of prey such as peregrine falcons.

It supports a breeding population of red grouse which depends on the health of the heather moorland, as grouse feed particularly on young heather shoots.

Heather moorland is a very threatened habitat which has been destroyed over many acres of Mid Wales by forestry or agricultural improvement, as you will see on much

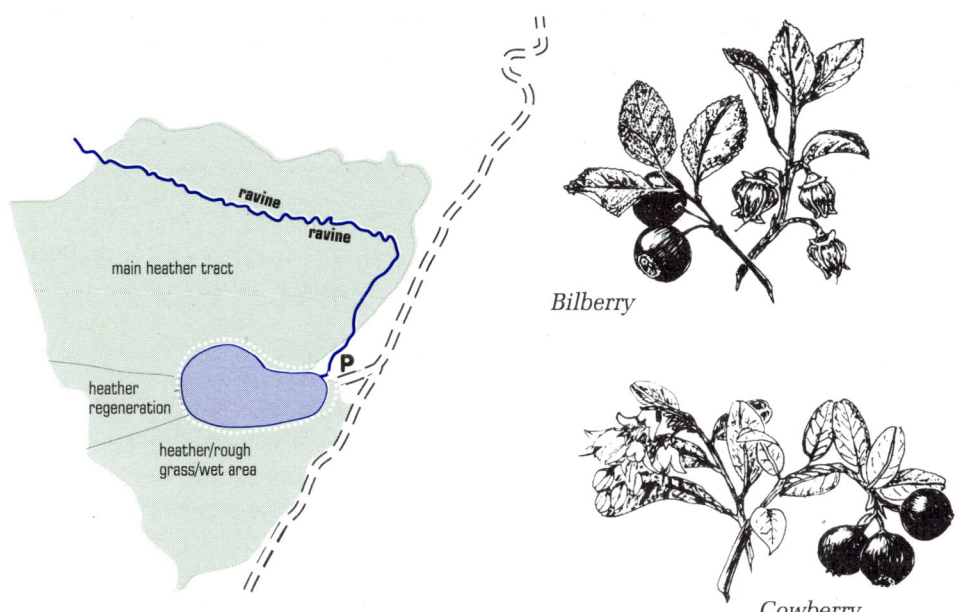

*Bilberry*

*Cowberry*

of the upland that is not protected by nature reserve status or management agreement. There are four members of the heather (or heath, *Ericaceae*,) family here – common heather or ling; bell heather with its cluster of purple bells towards the top of the stem; cross-leaved heath, similar in flower to bell heather but with leaves arranged in regular fours up the stem; and bilberry with its bell like flowers and purple berries. The superficially similar crowberry with its needle-like leaves and hard black berries is in a different family.

In amongst the extensive areas of bog moss (*Sphagnum*) look for the two insectivorous plants, sundew and butterwort, each equally distinctive in its own way. Sundew has red sticky hairs on rounded leaves to catch small insects, while the lime green rosette of leaves on butterwort turn in at the edges of their sticky surface to trap the unwary fly.

## Nearby Sites:

Those wanting a long trek through this wild upland countryside can continue along the approach track to the reserve in a roughly southerly direction right up onto the flank of Plynlimon, but it is not countryside for the inexperienced or unprepared. This is one of the ancient trackways across the hills.

For a comparison between the natural lake of Glaslyn and the artificially created reservoir, take the road around the Llyn Clywedog reservoir at Staylittle. There are many parking places, picnic areas and vantage points.

# 10 ~ Coed Gwernafon
## The Woodland Trust

*80 acres of first class semi-natural sessile oakwood, providing a delightful walk and protection for traditional wildlife, especially birds, of the Mid Wales uplands.*

### How to get there

Well hidden, but not far off the main road, leave the B4518, Llanidloes to Llanbrynmair road at the top of the hill overlooking the Clywedog reservoir towards Van. In about 1 mile turn left up the minor road to Llawryglyn. You enter the reserve over a cattle grid, but keep going almost to the next cattle grid before pulling onto the proper car park.

### What to See

This is another classic sessile oakwood, but differs from some in comprising a large amount of well spaced standards rather than old coppice stools, and relatively little shrub layer at present.

Since buying the wood in 1991 the Trust has excluded grazing sheep with almost a mile of fencing. This is allowing natural regeneration of the trees, which as well as oak include rowan (mountain ash), birch and, in the wetter areas, willow.

The carpets of moss on the steeper slopes and stream sides are indicative of the high grazing pressure in the past. Without the sheep, the bilberry, wavy

**Maps:** LR 136; PF 907; grid ref: SN 923903.

**Access:** Open at all times. Easy to medium walking on tracks and public footpaths.

**Parking:** A small car park has been created on the roadside at the southwest corner of the reserve.

**Public Transport:** Postbus from Llanidloes, Powys timetable 104.

**Contact:** Woodland Trust on 01476 581111.

**Facilities:** Guide leaflet.

**Time:** Allow 2 hours to explore the wood thoroughly.

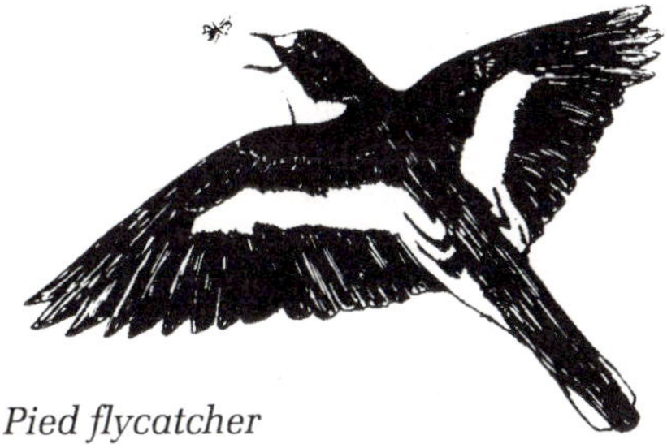

*Pied flycatcher*

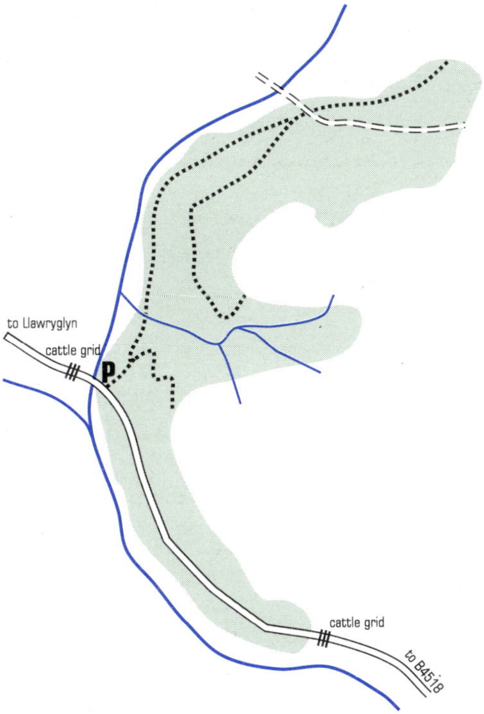


hair grass and other flowers of acid woodland can also grow taller.

The open aspect of the wood means there is a high chance of seeing as well as hearing the typical oakwood birds of summer – pied flycatcher, redstart and wood warbler – as well as the resident tits, woodpeckers and treecreepers.

Festival of the Countryside Mid Wales

## Nearby Sites

Back over the hill is the Clywedog Reservoir, which despite its artificial character offers much wildlife interest at various points on the road around the lake.

The Hafren Forest to the west of Clywedog provides acres of land for conifer loving species. You can follow the Severn up to its moorland source from the Forest Enterprise picnic area at Nant Melen.

For long distance walking opportunities there is Glyndwr's Way. For further details on this and other activities call at the Tourist Information Centre in Llanidloes.

# 11 ~ Llyn Mawr
## Montgomeryshire Wildlife Trust

*This 20 acre shallow upland basin lake is one of three lakes high on the moors above the Carno valley. It has a rich marginal flora illustrating the succession of water plants and is good for birds.*

**Maps:** LR 136; PF 908; grid ref: SO 011971.

**Access:** Open at all times. Access restricted to a narrow marginal zone which does not allow easy access right round the lake.

**Parking:** On the roadside verge but beware of ditch.

**Public Transport:** Caersws station 6km; bus every few hours on A470 3km, Powys timetable no 6.

**Contact:** MWT on 01938 555654.

**Facilities:** Leaflet to reserve.

**Time:** A brief visit will tell you whether there is much to see on the lake itself. Allow 1½ hours if you want to explore the lake side.

## How to get there

Turn north off the A470 about 2½ miles west of Caersws up the lane to Bwlch y Garreg. Follow the lane up – and up, almost as far as it goes. The lake and a bungalow appear on the left. Park on the roadside verge just before the bungalow. There is a stile and notice to an approach track.

## What to see

Unlike the deep lakes in hard rock basins, these shallow lakes fed off the moorland are much richer in nutrients and hence in vegetation and wildlife. Because the level of Llyn Mawr has been dropped slightly, it has a more extensive marginal zone of marsh and shallow water around its edge where bogbean, horsetail and yellow water lilies grow.

The reserve, embracing the lake and a narrow 10 acre strip of land around it, is rewarding at all times of year. The rich marsh vegetation includes a fine display of heath spotted orchids in June and you may find northern and early marsh orchids. Marsh cinquefoil adds its deep burgundy coloured flowers whilst amongst the moss and grasses are the insectivorous sundew and butterwort. Bog asphodel betrays its presence all the year, as yellow flowering spikes in summer or dead brown flower stalks that persist for most of the winter.

On the less accessible northern shore the process of plant succession can be seen as reed mace gradually takes over the shallow water, building up a platform of dead vegetation in which willow can become established. The so called willow carr itself dries out allowing invasion by birch and rowan.

This lake is a good site for birds in both summer and winter. There is a breeding colony of black-headed gulls, our commonest inland "sea gull", whilst breeding duck include mallard, teal and tufted duck. These are joined in the winter by pochard, wigeon, goldeneye and goosander.

Other summer breeders include great crested grebe – look out for them giving a pick-a-back to their young. Well hidden amongst the rushes and grass, snipe and curlew nest.

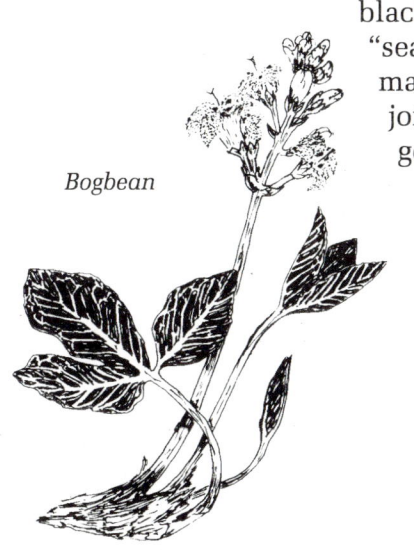

*Bogbean*

## Nearby Sites

There is an extensive network of bridleways that give access over the moorland and rough grazing of Mynydd Cerrigllwydian, one of which passes Llynytarw, another of the trio of Caersws lakes. This is good curlew country as well as offering hunting grounds for birds of prey including buzzard, kestrel and occasionally merlin and hen-harrier.

# 12 ~ Lake Vyrnwy
## Royal Society for the Protection of Birds

*Over 20,000 acres of woodland and moorland around the 3km long reservoir make this one of the largest and most varied reserves in Mid Wales – as well as a popular attraction.*

**Maps:** LR 125; PF 867.
Grid ref. SJ 020193.

**Access:** Road around the reservoir. Woodland paths and nature trails are always open.

**Parking:** Main car park by the dam at Llanwddyn.

**Public Transport:** None

**Contact:** RSPB on 01691 870278.

**Facilities:** Visitor centre, shop, toilets, disabled access to one hide and information area, scenic guide and three woodland nature trails. There are craft shops nearby.

**Time:** Short trail takes about ½ hour, but realistically, come for the day.

## How to Get There

There are several ways of reaching Lake Vyrnwy. Llanwddyn is served by the B4393 from the east and the B4396 from the north. For a really spectacular approach, come south over the Hirnant Pass from Bala. The single track road begins alongside a tumbling stream and ascends ever more steeply through the woods and out onto the moorland. It suddenly breasts the col and descends to the north end of the lake. Here choose either left or right on the road that runs right around the lake close to the water's edge.

## What to See

There is a certain irony in the fact that this reserve is a huge reservoir surrounded by large areas of coniferous woodland – neither habitat much favoured by conservationists.

Despite its visual attraction, the reservoir, as is often the case with such large and deep water bodies on acid rocks, is poor in nutrients and relatively lifeless. A few duck congregate in the sheltered bays. The presence of breeding goosander indicates an adequate supply of fish. In the winter more wildfowl come in to roost, along with gulls.

The conifer plantations, like the reservoir, may be reviled by the purists. But the trees enjoy that majesty that comes with age, and they do encourage species that favour conifers. Indeed they are a stronghold of the declining red squirrel population, and have allowed the build up of polecats to the point where these are now spreading outwards across the Welsh border. They also attract a breeding population of crossbills and siskins.

*Polecat*

The rocky streams that tumble down from the moorland, through the forest to the reservoir are perhaps the most 'natural habitat'. They are the haunt of those two characteristic birds of the upland streams: the grey wagtail (of which the most conspicuous feature is its yellow rump!) and the dipper. Both are feeders on the large insect population.

The main stream on the north bank flows into the lake close to the site of the old village of Llanwddyn which was drowned by the construction of the reservoir.

The moorland areas are attractive to birds of prey, and the mosaic of woods and moor gives the reserve a particularly high count of raptors. This is also curlew country, where the haunting trill of returning birds is a sign of spring. Ring ouzel, wheatear and golden plover migrate from even further afield to breed on these heather covered tops.

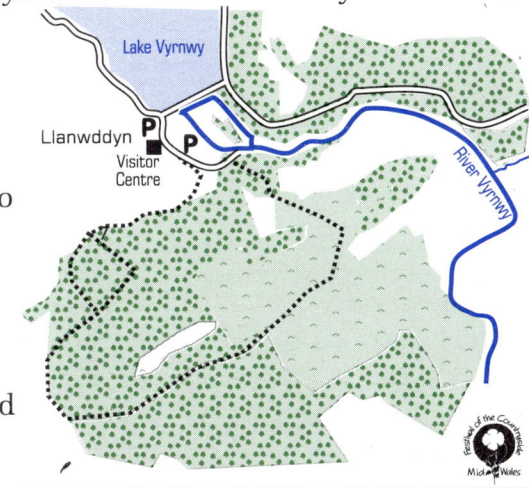

## Nearby Sites

Most spectacular beauty spot and attraction in the hills to the north of Vyrnwy is the waterfall of Pistyll Rhaeadr, at the end of the road from Llanrhaeadr-ym-Mochnant.

To the south, in late spring and early summer, make your way to the Montgomeryshire Wildlife Trust reserve at Dyfnant Meadows (grid ref. SH 999155). Not the easiest reserve to find, but a remarkable survival of unimproved hay meadows surrounded by plantations.

# 13 ~ Coed Pendugwm
## Montgomeryshire Wildlife Trust

*This 8 acre wood of mature beech and oak preserves the type of woodland once common throughout Wales but now much reduced by poor management, conversion to conifers or clear felling.*

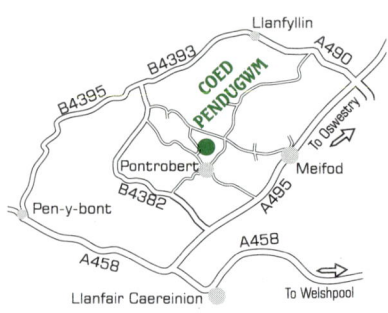

**Maps:** LR 125; PF867; grid ref: SJ 103142.

**Access:** Open at all times on winding paths through the wood.

**Parking:** Outside wood down the signed track opposite Pendugwm Farm. Muddy when wet.

**Public Transport:** None.

**Contact:** MWT on 01938 555654.

**Facilities:** Leaflet to reserve. Trail through the wood.

**Time:** Allow at least an hour to do justice to the trail.

## How to get there

From the A495 (Oswestry to Llanfair Caereinion road) two miles south of Meifod turn off into Pontrobert. At T junction by the bridge turn right then left for Llanfihangel. In about a mile, after sharp bend and a steep rise, you reach Pendugwm Farm. Turn down the track, remembering to shut the gate. Park on the reserve car park.

## What to see

This is another of those text-book woods, delightful yet unspectacular until you reflect on the fact that so few are left.

This is where you can go to be sure of seeing the once so common woodland plants – primrose, dog violet, wood anemone, then carpets of bluebells. Into the summer the trees, beech in particular, shade out some of the ground flora, but there are many less common plants to look for – early purple orchid, woodruff, common helleborine, yellow archangel and wild and barren strawberries indicate less acid soils than in some woods.

Mature trees and dead wood, deliberately left for the natural processes of decay by insects and fungi, provide plenty of food and nesting sites for the typical woodland birds such as great-spotted woodpecker, nuthatch and tree-creeper. As with many nature reserves the stock of "housing" is increased by the erection of nesting boxes.

Red squirrels are still seen occasionally, but it is the grey that you will most probably encounter. Badger and fox are known to use the reserve – see if you can pick up the distinctive musky odour of the latter – and otter have been recorded on the Nant-y-Pandy, the stream that borders the wood.

The exclusion of sheep has done wonders for the ground flora of this wood, where the acorns and beech mast are now able to germinate and new trees grow naturally.

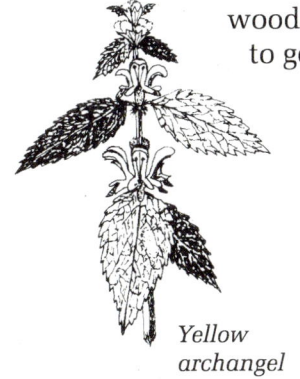
*Yellow archangel*

## Nearby Sites

When you have had enough of nature reserves, you can go and sample the tourist attractions of Llanfair Caereinion, including the Welshpool and Llanfair Light Railway. This gives a different perspective on the countryside as it runs close to the banks of the Afon Banwy.

On west side of the town an arboretum has been created from a patch of rough ground along the riverbank.

# 14 ~ Cwm-y-Wydden
## Montgomeryshire Wildlife Trust

*This nine acre oak wood on a north facing slope above the River Rhiw, preserves the typical semi-natural oak woodland flora and fauna of the area.*

**Maps:** LR 136; PF 887; grid ref: SJ 136025.

**Access:** A path through the wood, reached from a public footpath, is open at all times. It is very steep and rough in parts.

**Parking:** At cross roads by lane to Dinnant. Then walk up to wood.

**Public Transport:** None.

**Contact:** MWT on 01938 555654.

**Facilities:** Leaflet to reserve.

**Time:** Allow at least 1½ hours to reach the site and walk round the very steep trail.

## How to Get There

The wood is across the river to the south of the B4390 about 4 miles from Berriew and 2 from Manafon. At the very small cross roads park tidily, walk down the farm lane and over the river to Dinnant. The footpath goes left in front of the farmhouse, then half right to climb diagonally across the field to a stile that crosses into the corner of the wood. A circular path has been created up through the wood. There is no access to the portion of the reserve that runs down to the river bank.

## What to See

This is another fine though small remnant of sessile oak wood which was once so common on the valley sides. It is not wilderness – the characteristic growth of several stems from a single stump indicates active coppicing in the past – but human interference has not removed much of the wildlife. There is a marked difference in ground flora between the tangle of brambles on the west of the ravine and thin grasses with much cow-wheat to the east, reflecting past differences in management.

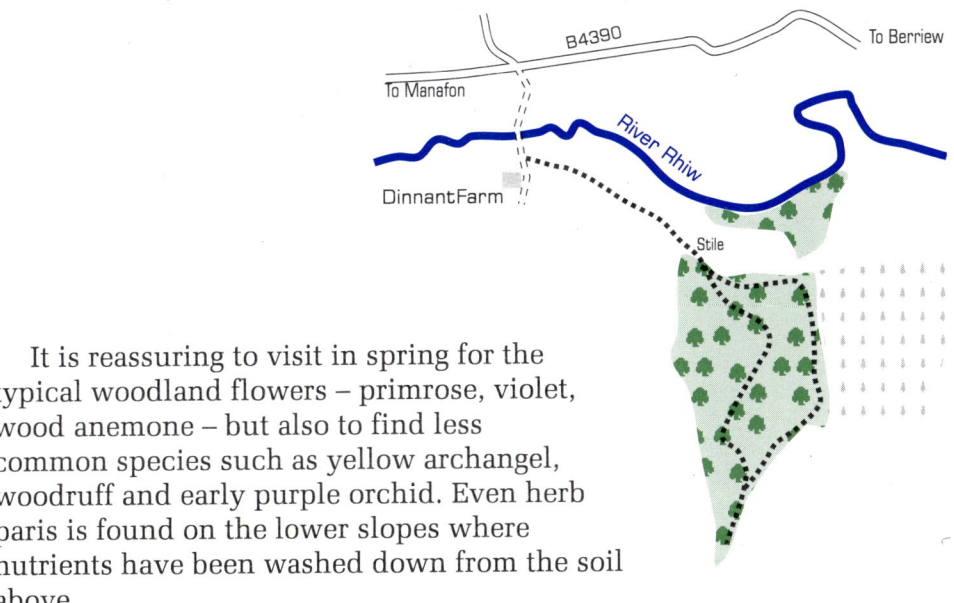

It is reassuring to visit in spring for the typical woodland flowers – primrose, violet, wood anemone – but also to find less common species such as yellow archangel, woodruff and early purple orchid. Even herb paris is found on the lower slopes where nutrients have been washed down from the soil above.

Speckled wood butterflies will dart ahead of you on the woodland ride, but you may not spot the purple hairstreak which keeps to the high canopy where its caterpillars feed on the oak leaves.

The small hole nesting birds – blue and great tits and pied flycatchers – appreciate a helping hand from the Trust, taking readily to nest boxes. Redstart and wood warbler, woodcock and tawny owl also breed while nuthatches, tree creepers and great spotted woodpeckers feed and breed in the dead and decaying wood.

It is a good mammal wood, though as usual you must rely more on tracks and signs than spotting the creatures themselves. The River Rhiw is used by otters, now on the increase.

*Speckled wood*

## Nearby Sites

The Montgomery Canal at Berriew is being restored to navigation, but is still a haven for wildlife. There is parking and a picnic area to the south of the village adjacent to the canal aqueduct. The River Rhiw is a good clean river with dipper and grey wagtail usually present.

# 15~Llanymynech Rocks
## Montgomeryshire Wildlife Trust

*This is border country, literally – the national boundary runs through the reserve where upland Wales meets lowland England and management is shared with the Shropshire Wildlife Trust.*

**Maps:** LR 126, PF 847; grid ref: SJ 265220.

**Access:** Open at all times. On Offa's Dyke National Trail and served by a number of footpaths.

**Parking:** At the end of the unmetalled lane on approach to reserve from north or in Llanymynech village to south.

**Public Transport:** Several bus services, inc. almost hourly D71 Oswestry to Llanymynech on A483.

**Contact:** MWT on 01938 555654.

**Facilities:** Leaflet to reserve.

**Time:** Allow at least 1½ hours to reach the reserve and wander round at leisure.

## How to get there

The reserve is close to the A483 Oswestry to Welshpool road, but rather well concealed. About 200m south of the Cross Guns take the small anonymous lane to the west opposite Rhiew Revel Lane. Follow round two bends and up to the end of the rough track where there is parking space.

## What to see

This reserve is a fascinating example of the healing power of nature. The limestone grassland and woodland that is now such a feature has all come in since quarrying of the Carboniferous Limestone stopped in the 1920s.

The steep quarry faces are themselves an important part of the reserve, providing nesting sites for the common jackdaw and the decidedly rare peregrine.

Weathered blocks of stone at the foot of the quarry faces clearly show the fossils of shelly animals that made up the limestone – most distinctive are the discs of limestone that formed the skeleton of crinoids (stone lilies, but animals despite their name). Look out also for the shells of brachiopods, the common "sea shells" of the time.

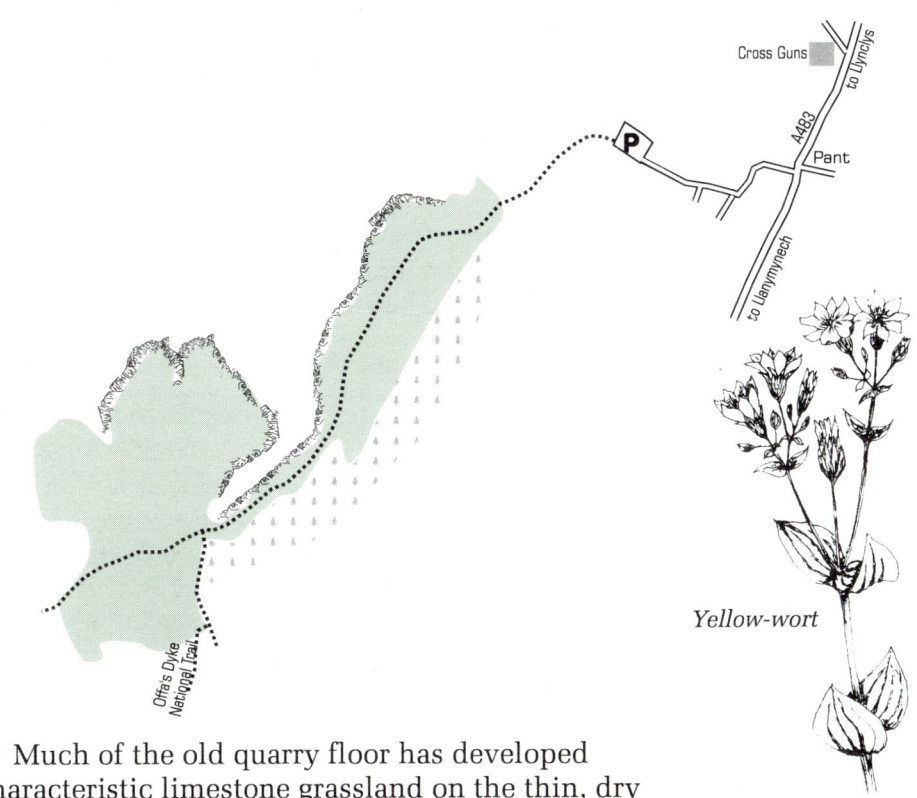

*Yellow-wort*

Much of the old quarry floor has developed characteristic limestone grassland on the thin, dry soil. The seasons are marked with a succession of flowers from the cowslips and early purple orchids, through the early summer flowering of spotted, pyramid and bee orchids accompanied by limestone lovers like milkwort and fairy flax. Later summer flowers include marjoram, yellow-wort and carline thistle, then the inconspicuous purple-pink trumpets of autumn gentian.

Butterflies are attracted to this riot of wild flowers. Particularly noticeable, though small, is the common blue.

Some of the vegetation is just too rampant here. A major management task is removal of the straggling wild clematis (traveller's joy or, in the winter, old man's beard), which otherwise tends to smother everything else.

## Nearby Sites:

Llynclys Hill, a northward continuation of the Carboniferous Limestone, where the extensive Common is managed as a reserve by the Shropshire Wildlife Trust.

The Montgomery Canal below the east side of Llanymynech Hill was the main means of transport for the limestone from 1796 to 1936. Now being restored to navigation but the best wildlife sites are being protected.

# 16 ~ Gaer Fawr Wood
## The Woodland Trust

*This 75 acre wood clothing a very prominent hill overlooking the Severn Valley offers a veritable catalogue of native broadleaved trees and shrubs as well as an interesting archaeological story.*

**Maps:** LR 126; PF 868; grid ref: SJ 2223128.

**Access:** Open at all times on public rights of way and paths that have been created. Some are a bit steep and muddy when wet.

**Parking:** At the quarry car park at the south west corner of the wood.

**Public Transport:** Bus services every few hours on route D71 Oswestry to Welshpool via Guilsfield.

**Contact:** The Woodland Trust on 01476 581111.

**Facilities:** Guide leaflet to reserve.

**Time:** Allow at least 1½ hours to walk around the whole wood and summit hill fort and admire the view.

## How to get there

From just north of Guilsfield on the Ardleen road (B4392) take the lane west, signed to Geuffordd. It climbs narrowly and steeply along the southern edge of the wood to the quarry car park on the right.

## What to see

The old quarry in which you park reveals the steeply dipping strata of hard grey shales and mudstone which underlie so much of central Wales. It is the rock dipping to the west combined with glacial erosion of the valley to the east that gives the distinctive profile to this hill, and left it as a naturally defensive site to be exploited by our Iron Age ancestors.

Gaer Fawr (the Great Camp or fort) refers to the hill top fort with its encircling ditches and ramparts. Within these the aim is to keep the area free of trees, as it would have been 2000 years ago. This is achieved by sheep grazing today, controlling regeneration and preserving a magnificent clear outward view across the Severn Valley to the Breiddens.

An internal fence controls the sheep and dramatically demonstrates the effect of grazing on the ground flora. Where sheep are excluded there is a dense undergrowth of brambles and shrubs or long grass.

Management of the wood has fluctuated over the years. In 1845 it was actively coppiced. This is seen in some magnificent multiple stems of oak and sweet chestnut. At the beginning of this century sheep were grazing throughout the wood, but now with controlled grazing there is regeneration of young trees and shrubs. In different parts of the wood these include oak, birch, ash, sycamore, sweet chestnut, hawthorn and hazel; but many other species are also found. Above the outermost rampart there is holly. Look out also for field maple and lime as well as Scots pine, the last probably a late Victorian addition.

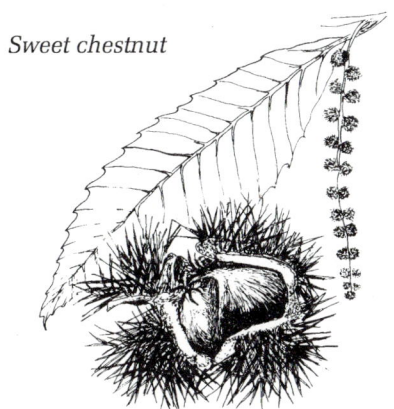

*Sweet chestnut*

This variety of species and woodland structure leads to an equal wealth of insect and bird life, with nuthatch, treecreeper and spotted flycatcher amongst the trees while skylarks rise from the open areas.

## Nearby Sites

The area is well served by public footpaths. Longer walks can be devised that will take you up to Gaer Fawr wood and the surrounding area.

Two miles to the east a branch of the Montgomeryshire Canal that once ran to Guilsfield is being developed as an "off line" nature reserve – a refuge for some of the special plants that will be at risk when the main line of the canal is restored to navigation.

The prominent Breidden Hills across the Severn are composed of an alkaline volcanic rock which not only gives them a very distinctive flora but is also valuable roadstone, leading to another conflict of interest.

# 17~Llyn Coed y Dinas
## Montgomeryshire Wildlife Trust

*A splendid example of opportunistic creation of a nature reserve in 1994. The lake was a gravel pit for the by-pass, then allowed to flood. It has proved a great attraction for wetland wildlife.*

**Maps:** LR 126; PF 888; grid ref: SJ 222053.

**Access:** Open during daylight hours. Free access to path round meadow and to hide.

**Parking:** Reserve car park on site off A490, 100m north of the junction with the A483.

**Public Transport:** Bus service D75 between Welshpool and Newtown. Train, 1½ miles from Welshpool.

**Contact:** MWT on 01938 555654.

**Facilities:** Large hide and exhibition overlooking lake. Educational visits arranged for groups.

**Time:** Drop in for a quick look at what is there. You may find yourself staying two hours at interesting times.

### How to get there

Easily accessible, Llyn Coed y Dinas is two miles south of Welshpool at the point where the A483 (by-pass) joins the old main road (A490). Go 100m up the A490 towards Welshpool centre from the junction and turn into the clearly marked reserve car park.

### What to see

A well laid path suitable for wheelchair and push-chair use takes you through a 'heathy' corner, planted up with gorse. You pass between a strip of embryo woodland (designed to cut off disturbance from the main road as it develops) and a meadow where appropriate mowing will encourage those grasses and flowers most beneficial to insects. A natural hollow, excavated and flooded to give a marsh fringed pond, was soon colonised by an array of aquatic insects.

Across a ditch the path takes you to the hide – and what a hide! This is a real de luxe model giving a magnificent view over the water. But the highlight from March until August is the sand martin colony close to the north window. In an inspired moment of habitat creation a 'cliff' was left in the

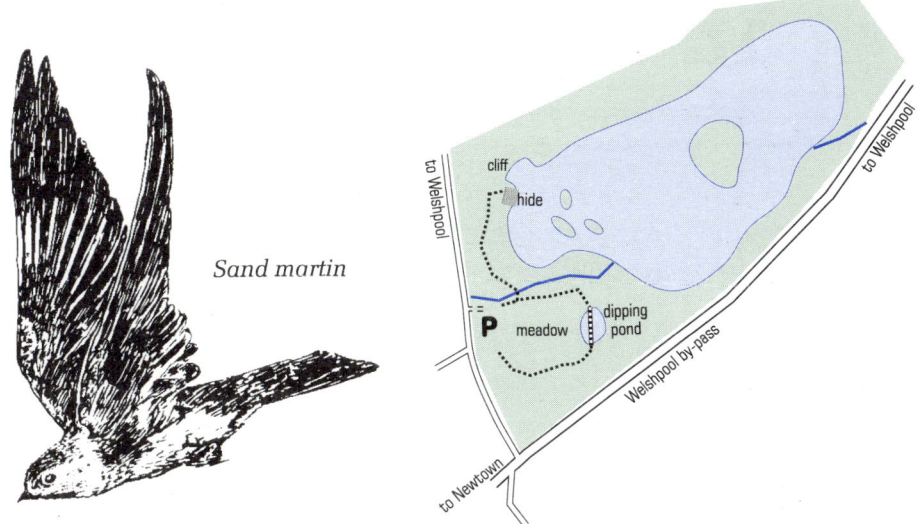

*Sand martin*

gravel. Unperturbed by construction work the sand martins returned in 1995 to set up a thriving colony. Coots, Canada geese, great crested grebe and little ringed plover have also made themselves at home in the summer. In the winter the familiar mute swan is joined by the whooper swan from Iceland, Scandinavia or Russia. Wigeon winter here along with resident mallard and tufted duck and the duck population will doubtless grow as the site becomes established.

The lake has a connection at wetter times with the River Severn, easily forgotten on the far side of the by-pass. Fish, invertebrates and fragments of plant material will come in naturally from the river. But to give nature a helping hand a number of different marginal habitats have been planted with reedmace, rushes and bur-reed.

## Nearby Sites

Llyn Coed y Dinas is a valuable addition to a chain of good wetland sites down the Severn Valley from Llanidloes to the Vyrnwy confluence on the national boundary. Here the flooded water meadows around Melverley are a splendid place to view wildfowl in the winter.

In the centre of Welshpool the Montgomeryshire Wildlife Trust have created another wetland reserve at Severn Farm Pond, giving the opportunity, especially for educational purposes, to illustrate the wealth of wildlife that can become established in urban surroundings.

Good quality still water habitat is provided by the Montgomery Canal, which runs parallel to the Severn from Welshpool to near Newtown. A pleasant stretch at Belan locks is reached down the lane just across the A490 from the reserve.

For the wildlife of ancient parkland, or just for the attraction of the historic castle and its splendid gardens go towards Welshpool and into the National Trust's Powis Castle.

# 18 ~ Dolydd Hafren
## Montgomeryshire Wildlife Trust

*The River Severn (Afon Hafren) loops lazily across its relatively flat glaciated valley floor here. Its loops and bends have formed oxbow lakes which are now good wetland habitat for waterfowl.*

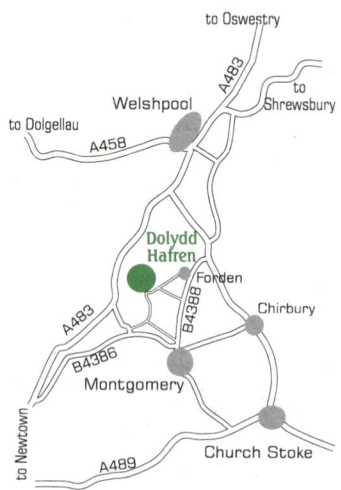

### How to get there

The reserve is on the east side of the Severn between the river and the centre of Forden village off the B4388 (Montgomery to Welshpool road). Through Forden village keep going for about 1½ miles to the Gaer farm at a sharp left bend. Turn right off the bend and down the track (can be muddy in winter) to the reserve car park. Keep to the footpath which leads to the observation hides.

### What to see

Like many riverside wetland sites, the winter is the best time to visit here, when waders and wildfowl are clustered along the water's edge or in the shallows. On the stubble of the adjacent fields large flocks of skylarks and yellow hammers may be feeding.

The site is proving attractive to otters. The best chance to see them is from the hide furthest from the car park.

In the spring sand martins, common sandpiper and little ringed plover return from foreign parts.

The structure of the reserve is of interest here. As a river like the Severn works its way down through the gravels of its flood plain, it does so in a series of

**Maps:** LR 126/137; PF 888; grid ref: SJ 208005.

**Access:** Open at present August to March; closed April to July to avoid disturbance to breeding birds.

**Parking:** On the reserve car park at the end of the approach lane.

**Public Transport:** None.

**Contact:** MWT on 01938 555654.

**Facilities:** Two observation hides.

**Time:** Allow at least two hours to enjoy all the site has to offer.

great loops, eroding material from the outside of the bend and depositing it on the inside. Thus the pattern of loops tends to move downstream, snake-like. Occasionally one of the loops breaks through at the neck and the main part of the loop remains as a cut-off oxbow lake. Old oxbows account for the complex pattern of wet hollows incised into the riverside meadows. The Trust has dredged out some pools to give more standing water.

On the surrounding fields look out for "mad March" hares – at any time of year – and the occasional peregrine sweeping across in the hope of picking up a meal, perhaps of a pigeon feeding on the seed.

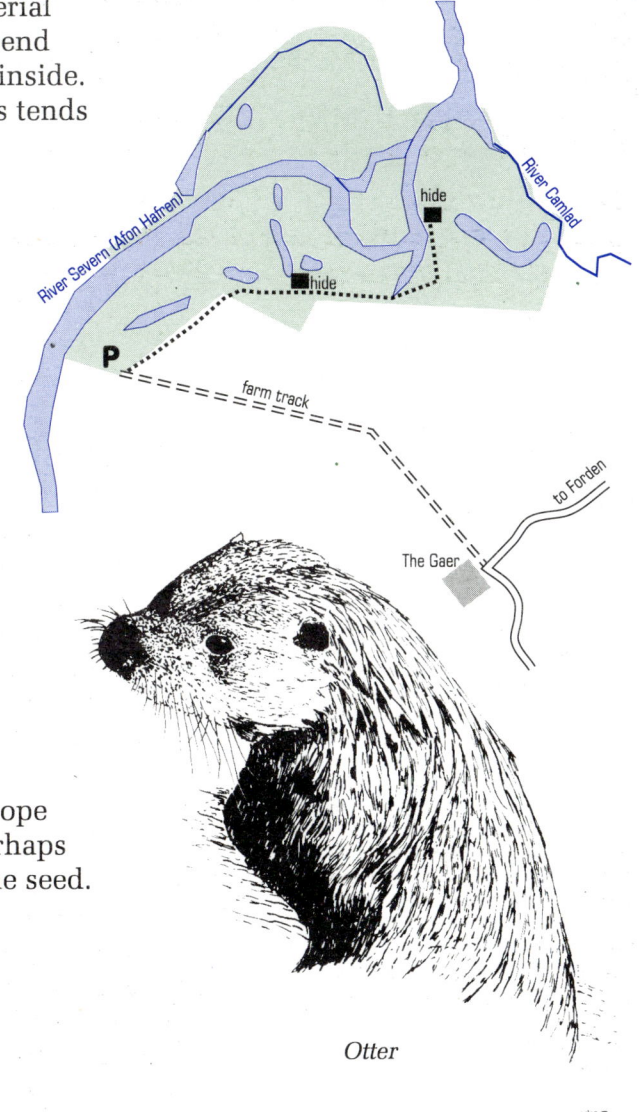

Otter

## Nearby Sites

Dolydd Hafren is one of a number of key wildlife sites that have been identified on the River Severn between Llanidloes and the Welsh border at Melverley. One is already a nature reserve – Llyn Coed y Dinas (see previous entry). Another is taking shape at Pwll Penarth, a few miles downstream towards Newtown. Access arrangements are not finalised for the whole reserve, but you can reach Penarth Weir by footpath along the bank of the Montgomery Canal.

# 19 ~ Roundton
## Montgomeryshire Wildlife Trust

*This prominent craggy hill of volcanic rock offers a wide range of habitats for animals and plants, from woodland around the base through unploughed hill grassland to exposed rock faces.*

**Maps:** LR 137; PF 909; grid ref: SO 293947.

**Access:** Open at all times; with marked trails around the reserve but the longer one very steep and rough.

**Parking:** Car park just within the reserve gate.

**Public Transport:** None.

**Contact:** MWT on 01938 555654.

**Facilities:** Information sign and car park.

**Time:** Allow at least two hours to get right around the trail.

## How to get there

Roundton is one of the best sign-posted nature reserves in this book. Brown and white tourist signs direct you off up either of two lanes from the A489 east of Churchstoke. Follow the signs to the reserve where there is an ample car park inside; but please remember to <u>shut the gate</u>.

## What to see

The best way to take in all features of interest is to keep to the waymarked path. It starts with a small pond, an addition to the habitats soon after the reserve was bought in 1985. It has a good display of monkey flower (*Mimulus*) an escape from cultivation which has naturalised well in recent years.

Over the stile the path goes through the ash, oak and rowan woodland (with some invasive sycamore) that occupies the lower slopes. Look out here for the green woodpecker, which may not be pecking wood but could be digging up an ant-hill.

If you don't want the steep climb of the whole walk, turn back when the path crosses the stream. To complete the circuit cross out onto the lane and back onto the reserve about 400 metres further up. There is a steep climb to the hill-fort crowned summit, where crags also reveal the volcanic nature of the hill's past. The very thin soil dries quickly in the summer. The hill is therefore well known for its spring ephemerals – that group of short lived annual plants that grow and flower early at the beginning of the season – which include shepherd's cress, vernal whitlow grass and upright chickweed.

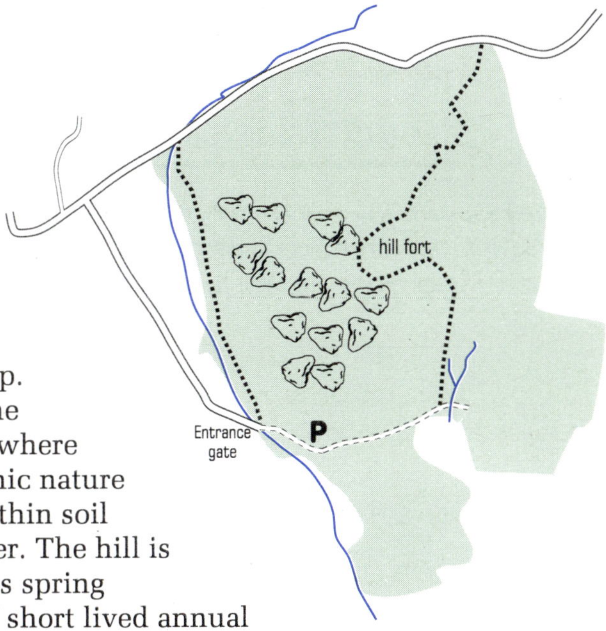

The adits (tunnels) of the old barytes (barium sulphate) mines are a feature of the reserve and, as well as hollow trees, provide roosts for bats.

The Trust is trying to restore the southern part of the reserve to woodland, as it was before being devastated by Dutch elm disease.

*Mimulus*

## Nearby Sites

Roundton is in a "peninsular" of Wales, projecting into England. Many of the nearby places of interest (even to the west) are across the border in Shropshire. Try a walk out northwards, past (or up if you are energetic) Corndon and on to Stapeley Hill with its stone circle of Mitchell's Fold. The lane east from Chirbury gives access to the footpath along Marrington Dingle, an impressive wooded valley where the River Camlad occupies a glacial overflow channel.

# 20 ~ Coed Rheidol
## Countryside Council for Wales

*Best known for the Devil's Bridge falls on the Afon Rheidol, the sessile oak woodland that clothes the gorge is a National Nature Reserve important for its mosses, ferns and birds of rapid streams.*

## How to get there

Finding Coed Rheidol is easy – Devil's Bridge has been a favourite tourist attraction for over a century. Take the A4120 – the scenic alternative between Ponterwyd and Aberystwyth, or if you are in the Rhayader area take the mountain road over to Cwmystwyth and then B4574. Public footpaths give access to many parts of the Gorge; but do take care and keep to official footpaths at all times. The private woodland, which you pay to enter, is not included within the National Nature Reserve, though much is as spectacular.

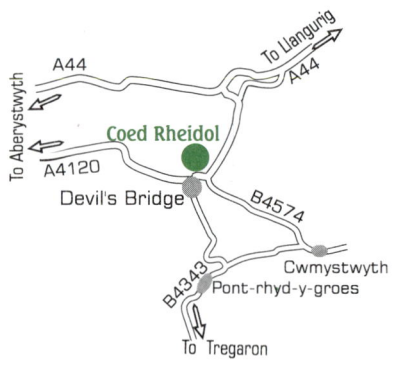

**Maps:** LR 135; PF 947; grid ref: SN 711785 to 739785.

**Access:** Open via public footpaths, but many are steep and require extreme caution.

**Parking:** In Devil's Bridge.

**Public Transport:** Trains from Aberystwyth during the summer on Vale of Rheidol Railway. Postbus service no. 596.

**Contact:** CCW warden on 01974 831671.

**Facilities:** None.

**Time:** This is a place to come to at your leisure and explore for half a day or more.

## What to see

This is a magnificent stretch of ancient sessile oak woodland, protected largely by its inaccessibility, hanging precariously on the flanks of the gorge of the Afon Rheidol.

The naturally high rainfall and the local micro-climate created by the spray from the falls at the foot of the narrow gorge contribute to high humidity, and a resulting abundance of the non-flowering plants – mosses, liverworts, lichens and ferns. They clothe the trees, the ground and the rocks in a variety of

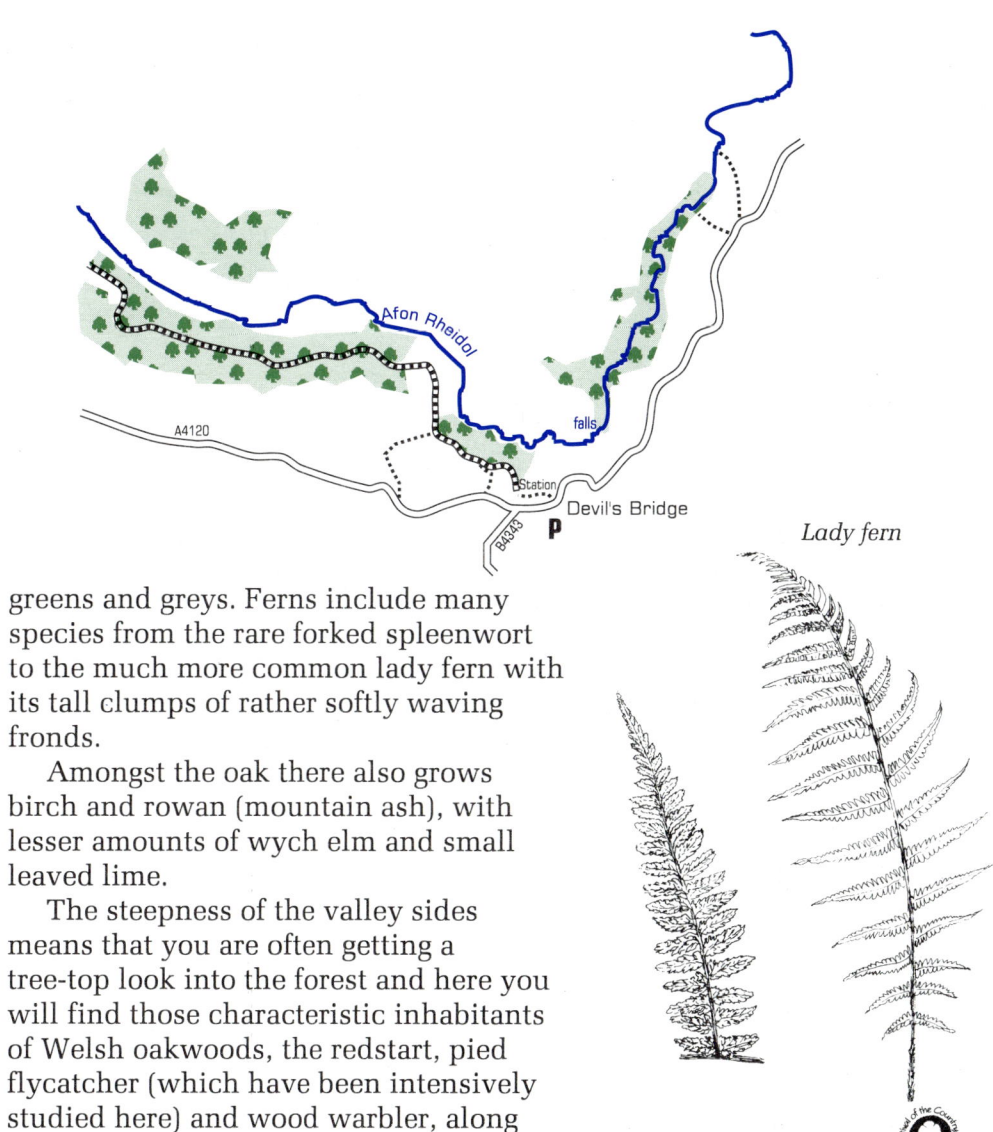

*Lady fern*

greens and greys. Ferns include many species from the rare forked spleenwort to the much more common lady fern with its tall clumps of rather softly waving fronds.

Amongst the oak there also grows birch and rowan (mountain ash), with lesser amounts of wych elm and small leaved lime.

The steepness of the valley sides means that you are often getting a tree-top look into the forest and here you will find those characteristic inhabitants of Welsh oakwoods, the redstart, pied flycatcher (which have been intensively studied here) and wood warbler, along with the resident blue and great tits.

## Nearby Sites

There is a lot of "Wild Wales" around Devil's Bridge. Taking the B4574 to Cwmystwyth you will pass forest walks in Hafod. Follow this road further and it becomes a moorland mountain road over the tops to the Elan Valley.

Forest Enterprise have clothed much of hillside around here, but the extent to which that reduces its "wildness" is a matter of opinion. Forestry is put on show at the Nant yr Arian Forest Visitor Centre on the A44, which offers a splendid panorama down the Arian valley and a wide variety of walks.

# 21 ~ Cors Caron
## Countryside Council for Wales

*This extensive "raised bog" has been used over the centuries for grazing of stock and peat digging, but is still a wild area of sufficient importance to be a National Nature Reserve.*

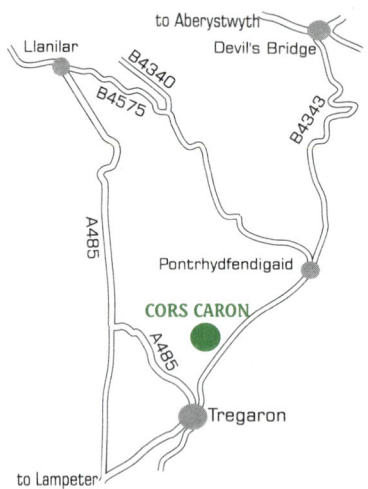

**Maps:** LR 135, and 146; PF 968; grid ref: SN 690640.

**Access:** Open to all on the walk along the Old Railway, which is suitable for wheelchairs. Permit available for other paths.

**Parking:** Car park off the B4343, 3 miles north of Tregaron.

**Public Transport:** Bus 588, 561, 562

**Contact:** CCW Warden on 01974 831671.

**Facilities:** Walk along the track of a disused railway line. Observation tower. Riverside trail by permit. Educational facilities by permit.

**Time:** Allow at least two hours to walk all the Old Railway Track and back from the car park.

## How to get there

Cors Caron or Tregaron Bog occupies much of the land immediately west of the B4343 between Tregaron and Pontrhydfendigaid. There is a public access point at the north end at Ystradmeurig (grid ref. 711672). Better parking is in the signed car park on the B4343, three miles north of Tregaron.

## What to see

At first sight, acres of rather dull looking peat bog! But in reality this is rather a special place – special enough for its 2000 acres to be declared a National Nature Reserve.

The main points of the story are told on a series of panels between the car park (once a goods loading bay on the Milford to Manchester railway) and the lookout tower which gives a fine view over the bog.

From the track you can see that parts of the bog surface are slightly domed. This is the result of accumulation of plant material, particularly species of bog moss (*Sphagnum*) over the past 10,000 years since the valley floor was levelled by glaciers of the last Ice Age.

These raised areas now receive all their water from rain, and have become

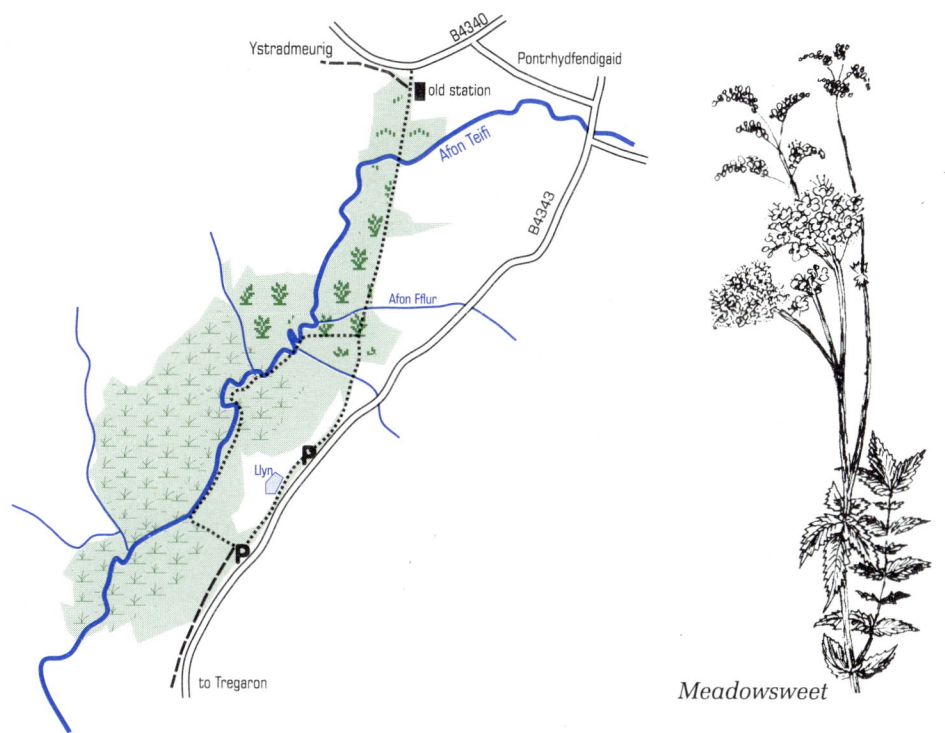

*Meadowsweet*

very acid with a characteristic flora of heather, cross-leaved heath and cotton grasses. The last, with their distinctive white fluffy "flowers" are strictly sedges rather than grasses, distinguished by their triangular stems. The white beaked sedge grows through the *Sphagnum* in the hollows on top of the domes. This sedge is the main food plant of the large heath butterfly.

Around the domes is a zone of less acid ground where the vegetation includes the stiffly erect stalks of yellow-flowered bog asphodel, and the tall creamy clouds of meadowsweet in late summer.

In the summer there is a good array of breeding wetland birds but they tend to be inconspicuous, none more so than the skulking water rail. Many more birds come in during the winter including a flock of whooper swans which are less likely to be overlooked.

## Nearby Sites:

East of Pontrhydfendigaid are the ruins of Strata Florida abbey. From there you can follow a lane south eastward to the picnic area at Pantyfedwn (grid ref. 753650).

From Ffair-Rhos a lane, becoming no more than a mountain track, gives access for the energetic walker to the crags and pools of the high hills which feed the Afon Teifi.

# 22 ~ Dinas
## Royal Society for the Protection of Birds

*Embedded deep in the Mid Wales uplands, this is where you expect wild places; but in fact the reserve at Dinas preserves one of the few broadleaved woodlands in an expanding sea of conifers.*

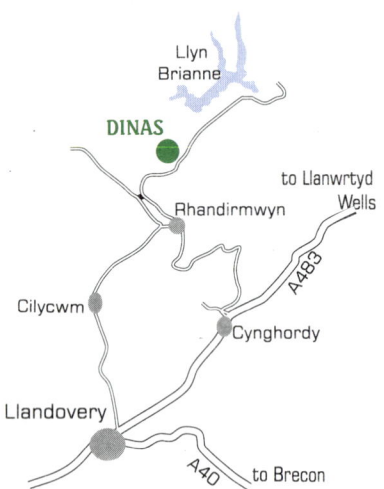

**Maps:** LR 147; PF 1013; grid ref: SN 788472.

**Access:** Dinas reserve open all year, but the info centre Easter-Sept only. Footpaths on a board-walk in part, some very rough ground, and some pleasant more or less level sections.

**Parking:** Car park at the main entrance; smaller parking space in a lay-by off the approach road.

**Public Transport:** None.

**Contact:** RSPB Wales Office on 01686 626678.

**Facilities:** Car park, information centre open weekends, Easter to September and daily in August, nature trail and guide leaflet.

**Time:** Allow 2 hours for a leisurely visit.

## How to get there

Best approach is from the A483 at Llandovery, or just north of Cynghordy, and through Rhandirmwyn village then follow signs to Llyn Brianne. The road is very narrow in places; proceed with due care. The main car park is just after the church, though the lay-by you come to first does give access to the wood.

## What to see

This is a splendid wood for its summer birds, which of course is why it is an RSPB reserve. It was here that the last red kites nested prior to their current recovery. The wood is now too much disturbed for kites, but they can often be seen wheeling overhead. Other birds of prey – buzzards, peregrines, kestrels and sparrowhawks – are also around in sufficient numbers to keep small birds and mammals on their toes!

The well spaced sessile oaks sporting a good growth of mosses and lichens typical of these moist Welsh woods are also home to a strong population of pied flycatchers, along with redstarts, tree pipits, wood warblers. There is a year-round presence of the "wood"

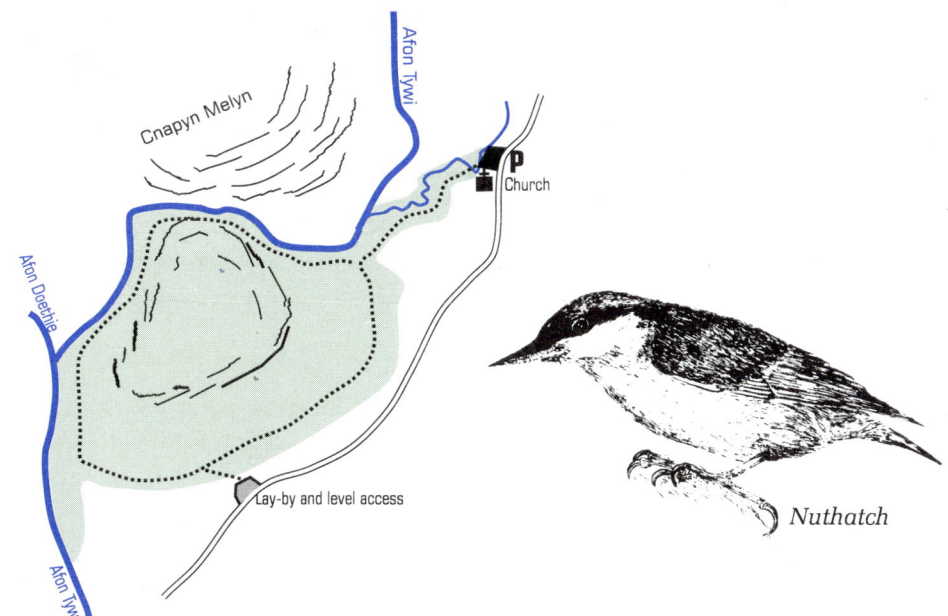

*Nuthatch*

birds – the three British woodpeckers, nuthatch and treecreeper.

Ground vegetation beneath the trees is somewhat sparse on the steep northern side of the reserve, but conspicuous amongst the thin woodland grasses is the anaemic yellow flower of cow-wheat, a plant that is semi-parasitic on grass roots.

Water also plays a vital part on the reserve. The first section of the trail from the car park is on boardwalks over marshy ground where the marsh marigold lives up to its name in early spring, with golden saxifrage and orchids later. The Afon Tywi half circles the reserve, rushing through a rocky gorge with spectacular scenery but access to this rougher part of the trail path is only for the sure footed. In the water you may spot salmon or trout and, feeding on them, family parties of goosander, one of the saw-billed ducks.

## Nearby Sites

Just downstream from Dinas, and arching across the hillside from the Gwenffrwd valley to the Afon Doethie is the RSPB's Gwenffrwd reserve. This is kept much quieter than the Dinas reserve and visitors are asked to go there only after reporting to the Dinas Information Centre.

The road above Dinas brings you to the dam of the Llyn Brianne reservoir whose thin fingers of water stretch far up the valleys amongst the hillside plantations. Some may see this as a conservationist's nightmare, but it is spectacular scenery, and encourages those species that positively prefer coniferous woodland. You can follow this narrow mountain road round eastwards and down alongside the Nant Irfon National Nature Reserve to Abergwesyn (see next two entries).

# 23 ~ Vicarage Meadows
## Brecknock Wildlife Trust

*High in the hills at Abergwesyn are a couple of fields that remain unimproved – undrained and unfertilised – thereby conserving the flowers of ancient grassland that are now such a rarity.*

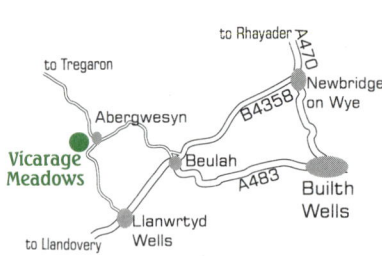

## How to get there

This is one of the most secluded sites in the book. A small cluster of farms and cottages that make up Abergwesyn lies 5 miles north of the A483 at Llanwrtyd Wells. There is limited roadside parking by the bridge over the Irfon. Take the driveway adjacent to the west bank of the river (not signed as footpath), past a cottage and the old graveyard, then right and through two gates onto the seven acre reserve.

## What to see

The first pasture is very wet in its lower part. Follow the most obvious paths through the grass and take care not to get stuck in waterlogged areas. Amongst the tussocks of purple moor grass is a wide variety of moisture loving species.

Beyond the line of tall beech trees, whose multiple trunks indicate they have grown out from a once laid hedge, is a much drier pasture. Early in the summer it is a mass of bluebells, but as these die down a host of other special meadow plants is revealed. Swathes of orchids (six species have been recorded here) poke up through the straggling branches of wood bitter vetch. The

**Maps:** LR 147; PF 991; grid ref: SN 850526.

**Access:** Open at all times, off public footpath. Can be wet and rough under foot.

**Parking:** On roadside by bridge over Afon Irfon.

**Public Transport:** Postbus, Powys timetable 100.

**Contact:** BWT on 01874 625708.

**Facilities:** None, though sign at reserve entrance tells you that you are in the right place.

**Time:** In late spring-early summer allow 1 hour to investigate the plants thoroughly.

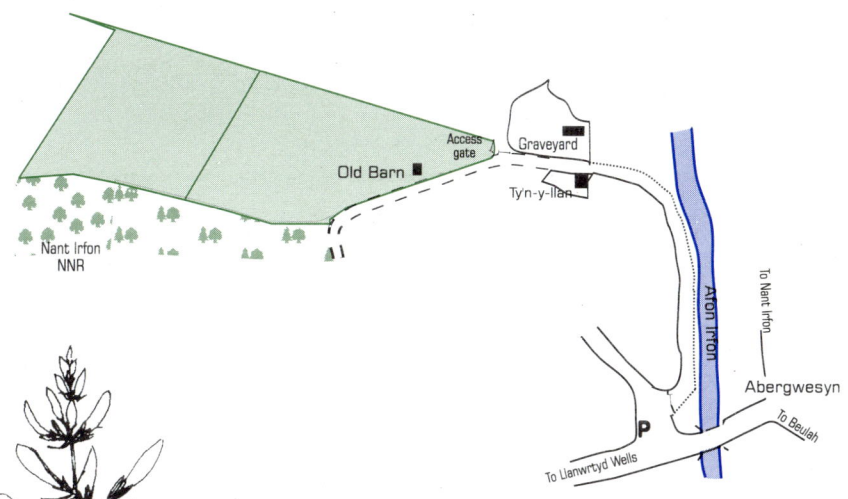

stunted yellow broom-like plant is dyer's greenweed, source of a traditional organic dye. There is also betony with its crown of purple trumpet flowers and scalloped leaves that look as though they were cut with scissors, and yellow rattle in later summer. This plant is partially parasitic on the grass roots that it grows amongst, and its seeds rattle in a flat pod at the end of the season.

*Dyer's greenweed*

The invasive clumps of downy birch in the lower pasture indicate the need for constant management with meadow sites such as this. The traditional management regime must be maintained and this means grazing the pasture after the flowering period. So later in the summer the plants are more difficult to spot and wet areas can become very muddy.

## Nearby Sites

Vicarage Meadows are adjacent to the Nant Irfon National Nature Reserve (see next entry) which can be reached over a stile in the fence of the upper pasture.

This is the heart of "Wild Wales" in terms of scenery, though largely tamed to a degree by agricultural improvement of the grazing land and planting of huge areas of conifers. The narrow but spectacular road from Abergwesyn goes north up the ice scoured valley of the Irfon then sweeps west and south through the Tywi Forest and round the flooded fingers of Llyn Brianne reservoir.

# 24 ~ Nant Irfon
## Countryside Council for Wales

*The National Nature Reserve occupies the steep western flank of the upper reaches of the Irfon. It is an area of largely open upland where birds of prey such as red kite, merlin and peregrine thrive.*

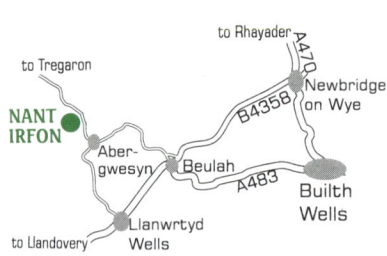

**Maps:** LR 147; PF 991; grid ref: SN 840546.

**Access:** Open but no recognised footpaths so difficult under foot.

**Parking:** On roadside by entry point at north end or in Abergwesyn to approach above Vicarage Meadows (see previous page).

**Public Transport:** Postbus to Abergwesyn; Powys timetable 100.

**Contact:** Countryside Council for Wales on 01874 730751.

**Facilities:** None.

**Time:** Allow plenty of time to stop and walk this reserve; or observe it from the road as you come down the Irfon valley.

## How to get there

Turn off the A483 at Llanwrtyd Wells or Beulah to Abergwesyn. At Abergwesyn take the mountain road to the Tywi Forest and Tregaron. The reserve comes down to the west bank of the river a few yards from the road for much of the way up the valley. At the northern end the road runs into the reserve and signs mark the entry point. Alternatively you can enter the reserve from above Vicarage Meadows (see previous page).

## What to see

Several habitats are encompassed within the reserve, though the greatest area is rough grassland. This open habitat needs the presence of grazing animals to maintain it, so a carefully controlled number of sheep graze the reserve. Unfortunately these do little to control the tussocky purple moor grass or the bracken which spread to the detriment of other wildlife. Cutting and chemical control are used on these plants in selected areas.

However, sheep are excluded from the sessile oak wood at the southern end of the reserve. This is growing near the upper limit of altitude for oak wood

*Red kite*

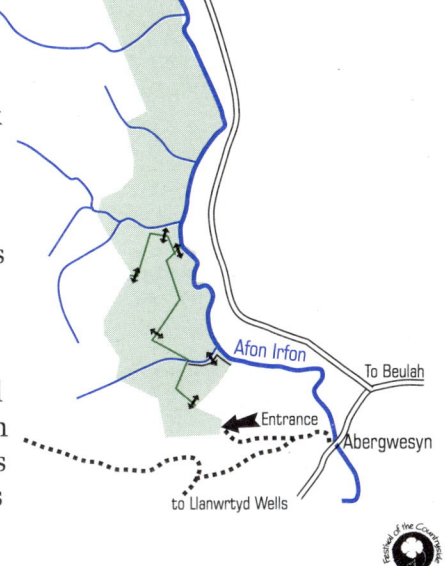

in Wales, and was likely to become very degraded because no natural regeneration occurred. Exclusion of sheep has allowed birch, rowan and oak seedlings to appear and the heavily grazed hazel bushes to sprout out.

Seasonal grazing from autumn through to spring is practised on the wet slopes running down from the oak wood to the river. This allows the summer meadow plants such as globeflower to flower and set seed.

By these means a mosaic of habitats is maintained which helps provide for the needs of a wide range of birds. This is one of the most ornithologically important areas of hill land in Wales. Along with Abergwesyn Common to the east, it certainly makes a striking contrast with the huge areas of conifer plantation to the west.

## Nearby Sites

At the information centre in Llanwrtyd Wells see live pictures in the summer from red kite and goshawk nests. The goshawk is one of the few beneficiaries of the conifer plantations. From October to April, Dol y Coed park at Llanwrtyd Wells is one of the kite feeding stations.

Forest Enterprise provide two picnic sites and forest walks on the road south from Abergwesyn.

# 25 ~ Elan Valley
## Dŵr Cymru Welsh Water

*Not so much a nature reserve as a vast tract of upland where, apart from water gathering, the emphasis is on conservation of landscape and wildlife. The Elan Valley estate embraces the Claerwen NNR.*

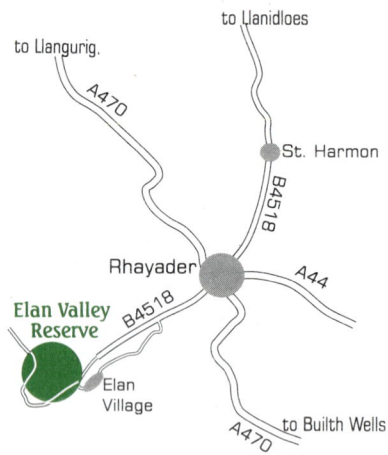

**Maps:** LR 147; PF 969; grid ref: SN 930648

**Access:** Open access to most of the estate, except the obviously fenced and private properties and works.

**Parking:** Ample car parks at Visitor Centre and many places around the reservoirs.

**Public Transport:** Postbus Powys timetable 103. Llandrindod Wells trains connect with bus in summer.

**Contact:** Elan Valley Visitor Centre, 01597 810880.

**Facilities:** Visitor centre with exhibition, shop, cafe, toilets, tourist information; over 70 miles of walks and trails described in leaflets; extensive programme of guided walks, birdwatching safaris etc.

## How to get there

Most will approach via the B4518 from the centre of Rhayader, but you can take the mountain route from the west via Cwmystwyth from Devil's Bridge. Starting point for your exploration should be the visitor centre below the Caban-coch dam.

## What to see

All the major upland habitats are represented within the 70 square miles of the Elan Valley Estate which is administered by Hamdden Ltd for Dŵr Cymru Welsh Water and the Elan Valley Trust.

Centre-pieces are the string of four late Victorian reservoirs up the Elan Valley and the huge Claerwen Reservoir officially opened in 1952. But these large water bodies are not in themselves very fertile or welcoming to much wildlife. A few duck and occasionally gulls congregate in the sheltered bays. Goosander may occasionally be seen in the summer. These sawbill ducks made this their first Welsh breeding site in 1971. Common sandpiper are attracted to the rather barren shores caused by the fluctuating water level.

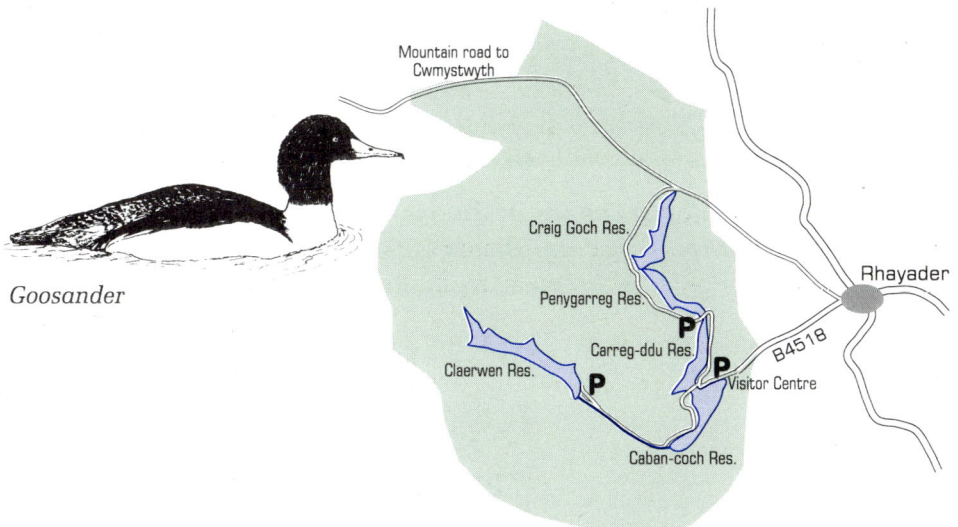

*Goosander*

There have been conifer woods here since the reservoirs were first built. Though often reviled by the purist they prove attractive to many birds. Kites and goshawks nest in them while smaller species favouring conifers include crossbills, goldcrest and siskin. There are some excellent ancient sessile oak woods clinging to the valley sides, which harbour very high densities of pied flycatcher and redstart.

The open moorland may appear monotonous and uninteresting but it is home to a surprising wealth of animals and plants. These rely on maintenance of the right conditions of drainage and grazing – sheep farming remains its primary land use, and over-grazing is a threat to many species. The moorland is tending to become invaded with purple moor grass at the expense of more varied but less aggressive plants. It was largely to control management of the blanket mire on easily eroded peat that a large area around the head of Claerwen was declared a National Nature Reserve in 1994. This is nesting ground for a few pairs of golden plover and dunlin. When voles are plentiful, short eared owls may sometimes be seen over the rough grassland.

## Nearby Sites

This site is so vast that you probably won't visit anywhere else the same day. But for information about what's on and where to go in the vicinity call at Rhayader Tourist Information Centre. Two nature reserves fairly near are listed in the next couple of entries.

The waters of the Afon Elan flow into the Wye which can be followed upstream to the source or down to its mouth (if you have the time!) on the Wye Valley Walk. Or cross the watershed over to Cwmystwyth and the beautiful woods of the Rheidol valley.

# 26 ~ Dyffryn Woods
## Royal Society for the Protection of Birds

*Right by the side of the main road this 77 acre wood is a good example of typical "hanging" broadleaved woodland on the valley side, with some open areas and rocky ravines.*

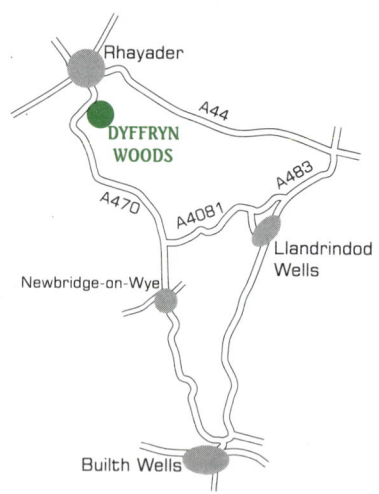

**Maps:** LR 147; PF 969; grid ref: SN 980672.

**Access:** Open at all times along a woodland walk, well maintained but steep in parts.

**Parking:** On A470 ½ mile SE of Rhayader.

**Public Transport:** Occasional bus between Rhayader and Builth Wells; Powys timetable 20.

**Contact:** RSPB Wales Office on 01686 626678.

**Facilities:** Waymarked walk.

**Time:** Allow 1½ hours to take a leisurely walk round the entire circular path.

## How to get there

One of the easiest reserves to find, being right alongside the A470 main road from Rhayader to Builth Wells. The wood is a conspicuous feature on the valley side. There is parking in a lay-by at the north end of the wood, from which a wicket gate opens straight onto the walk.

## What to see

No great surprises but there are good populations of the typical woodland summer visitors – pied flycatcher, wood warbler and redstart – as well as the resident tits, treecreepers, nuthatches and woodpeckers. At the top edge of the wood where it opens out onto gorse and bracken patches look (and listen) for the whinchat and stonechat with their clacking call note which gives the stonechat its name – and admire the splendid view west across to the hills above the Elan Valley. Whin incidentally is another name for gorse, and the bush which offers the whinchats' favourite song perch.

Most noticeable is the effect of management. The north end (Gigrin Wood) is open to the sheep that graze

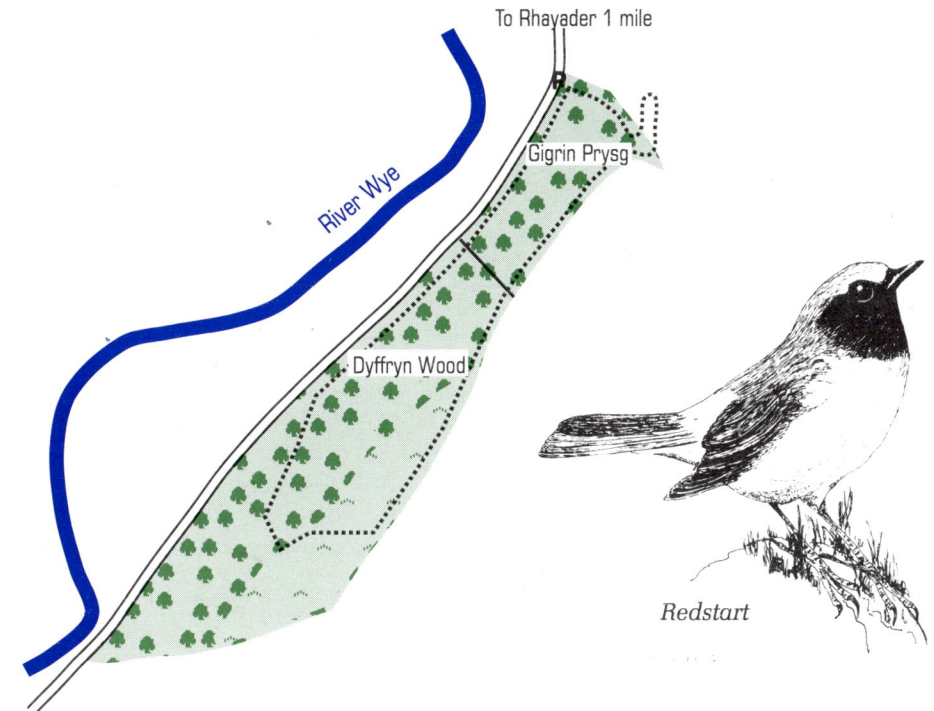

*Redstart*

on the pasture above. Ground vegetation is sparse. The greater part of the wood to the south is fenced off and there is abundant regeneration of the oak and silver birch.

The few rocky streams that cut notches into the otherwise uniform valley side support the two stalwarts, grey wagtail and dipper.

Walk quietly and you might see a polecat, or a common lizard basking in a patch of sun. Tracks and holes are the more likely evidence of the badgers and foxes that also live here but are mainly nocturnal movers.

## Nearby Sites

This is the heart of Kite Country. Gigrin Farm, signposted to the east between Dyffryn Wood and the centre of Rhayader, is the original kite feeding ground. Come here from October to March at 2.00pm and you can be sure of an amazing sight as several red kites as well as buzzard and raven drop in for a free meal. All year round there is a farm trail here, and a good chance that you will spot red kites soaring overhead from one of their nearby nesting sites.

There are many other "wild places" to explore – both the official nature reserves (see previous and following pages) and the attractive, but undesignated, surrounding countryside. Call in at the Tourist Information Centre in Rhayader for leaflets on walks including the upper reaches of the Wye Valley Walk which comes through the town.

# 27 ~ Gilfach Farm
## Radnorshire Wildlife Trust

*The whole-farm approach to wildlife conservation. Gilfach was a 383 acre (153ha) Radnorshire hill farm that had largely escaped modernisation, thereby preserving the traditional wildlife.*

**Maps:** LR 147; PF 948; grid ref: SN 965717.

**Access:** Unfenced land and farm trail open at all times. Farmhouse and its exhibition open Friday to Sunday, 10-5, April - Sept. Entrance fee payable for exhibition.

**Parking:** In lay-bys on the unfenced land or up at the farm.

**Public Transport:** None.

**Contact:** RWT on 01597 870301.

**Facilities:** Picnic area, farm trail, exhibition.

**Time:** This is a delightful spot at which to stop off for a picnic in passing. Allow 2 hours to explore the site, follow the trail and see the exhibition.

## How to get there

The reserve starts immediately across the cattle grid on the minor road to St Harmon about 3 miles north of Rhayader on the A44. To reach the farm house and exhibition follow the lane over the unfenced land and turn right just before the second cattle grid.

## What to see

The exhibition is only open seasonally on Fridays, Saturdays and Sundays, but the farm and the farm trail over the grounds are open at all times. You sense as much as see the difference between this farmed nature reserve and the more intensive agriculture that pervades the surrounding countryside. It is not neglected or abandoned to wildlife, but the pastures are a less vivid green than their heavily nitrogen-fed neighbours, the meadows are a mixture of many different grasses and wildflowers including globe flower and mountain pansy.

The field boundaries are still the old hedgebanks, reinforced with large blocks of lichen encrusted coarse slate. Indeed a number of nationally uncommon lichens are recorded here.

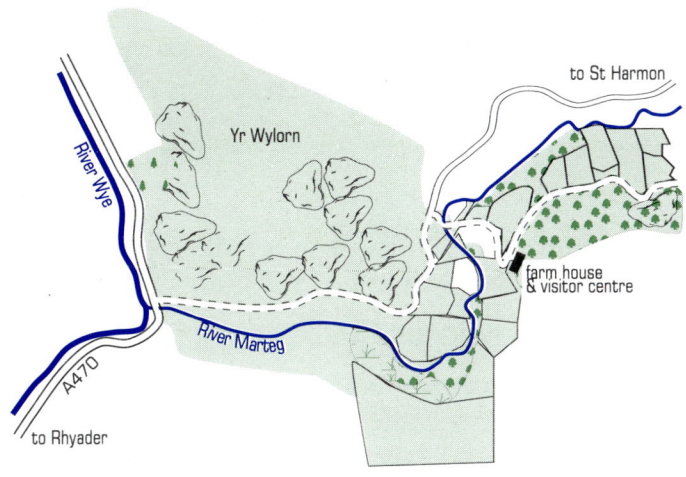

On the unfenced rough pasture wheatears flash their white rumps as they flit from crag to heather-sprouting crag. And in the sessile oak woods the pied flycatchers and redstarts can return summer after summer to sites which are still managed as they have been for hundreds of years. The only difference is that they, and several other species, will now be nesting under the watchful eye of a closed circuit TV camera which transmits pictures live to the exhibition centre during the breeding season!

To add to the variety of the habitat there is an old railway tunnel on the track of the long derelict line from Rhayader to Llanidloes in which live five species of bat. The low intensity farming also favours small mammals such as voles and thereby the population of birds of prey that feed on them.

*Mountain pansy*

## Nearby Sites

Rhayader is something of a centre for wild places, as the previous entries in this book show. But apart from these declared reserves there is much else to explore nearby. Call in at the Rhayader Tourist Information Centre to find out what's on.

The Wye Valley Walk passes through the reserve. Follow it as far as the mood takes you, towards the source or mouth. The whole of the river has been declared an SSSI.

This is Kite Country, the feeding station is just south of Rhayader, so these majestic birds may be spotted anywhere in the vicinity.

# 28 ~ Bailey Einon
## Radnorshire Wildlife Trust

*This reserve is 11 acres of steeply sloping deciduous woodland on the left bank of the River Ithon at a point where it cuts dramatically through the hills in a glacially eroded channel.*

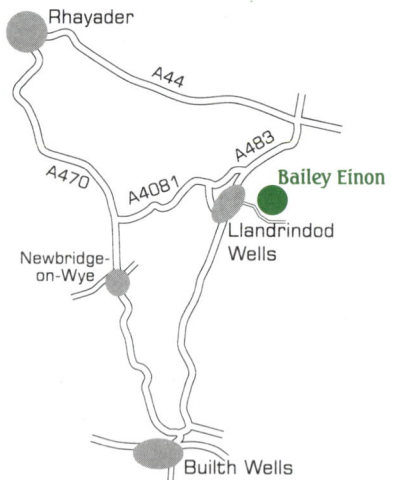

**Maps:** LR 147; PF 970; grid ref: SO 083613

**Access:** Open at all times along a maintained pathway, but some sections very steep and wet at times.

**Parking:** On the picnic site car park at the Shaky Bridge entrance to the reserve.

**Public Transport:** Bus and train at Llandrindod Wells, 1½ miles.

**Contact:** RWT on 01597 823298.

**Facilities:** Path through the wood.

**Time:** Allow 1½ hours to walk right through the reserve and back.

## How to get there

From the centre of Llandrindod Wells take Craig Road which passes out through expanding housing development to become Cefnllys Lane. There is a dramatic change in landscape as you breast the ridge and drop steeply into the gorge of the Ithon. Park where the road comes almost to the river at Shaky Bridge.

## What to see

This reserve has the immediate atmosphere of "a good wood" with long tailed tit, tree creeper, wren, great tit and green woodpecker greeting one (if lucky) within the first few yards. The path, in reasonable condition, rises to the upper fence line, with steps that are narrow and moderately steep. There are views out through the trees across to the church and the castle earthwork.

There is a good mix of native broad-leaved trees – oak with a shrub layer of previously coppiced hazel and field maple on the drier parts and ash/alder woodland in the wetter areas on the lower slopes and edge of the river flood plain.

These species support many insects including a number of uncommon

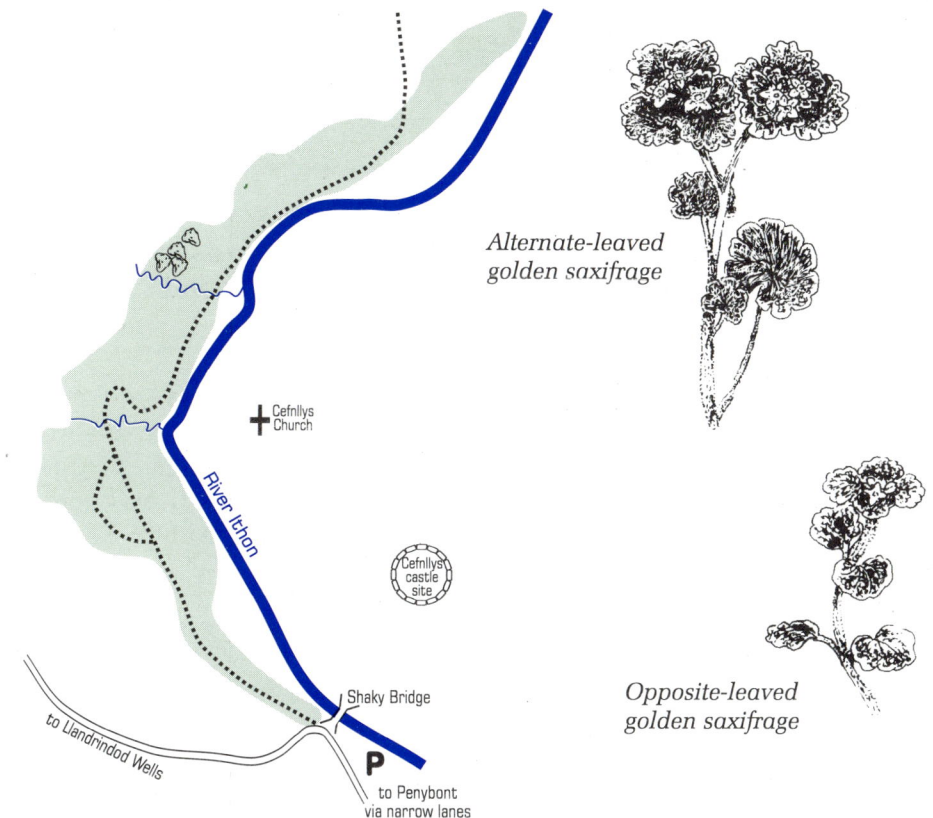

*Alternate-leaved golden saxifrage*

*Opposite-leaved golden saxifrage*

beetles such as three types of cardinal beetle and an unusual longhorn.

In the wet flushes where streams run down through craggy ground you will find both alternate-leaved and opposite-leaved golden saxifrage – distinguished as the names suggest by examination of the arrangement of leaves on the stalk.

## Nearby Sites

A public footpath continues the walk from the north end of the reserve towards Penybont. There is a forest walk in the very attractive mixed woodland south of the picnic area at Shaky Bridge.

The Radnorshire Wildlife Trust has two other reserves in the vicinity, of interest to the more dedicated naturalist. Abercamlo Bog at grid ref. 074650 is a place of structural interest. The three small basin mires are known as pingos – depressions caused by the collapse of "blisters" of ice formed during periglacial conditions at the end of the last Ice Age. Other similar frost heaving effects are clearly visible in the hummocky landscape as you approach the site west along the A44 from Crossgates then south down Gravel Road towards Llanyre.

Sidelands is a very small wood of mixed broadleaved species, tucked into the farmed landscape between Penybont and Crossgates off the A44 at grid ref. 107644.

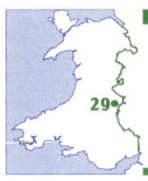

# 29 ~ Burfa Bog
## Radnorshire Wildlife Trust

*At first glance an unspectacular reserve, but how many places still show this splendid mosaic of wet and dry grassland habitats, alder carr and undrained pasture? Its 23 acres are a step back in time.*

**Maps:** LR 148, PF 971; grid ref: SO 275613

**Access:** Open at all times. Marked trail with boardwalk and bridges to get you around the reserve, but difficult to negotiate in parts.

**Parking:** On roadside near reserve entrance.

**Public Transport:** None.

**Contact:** RWT on 01597 823298.

**Facilities:** Reserve leaflet; trail around site.

**Time:** Allow 1 hour to walk round the main circuit on the reserve.

## How to get there

Take the minor road to Evenjobb, north off the B4594 Presteigne to New Radnor road at Ditchyeld Bridge and park on the roadside by the reserve entrance in about 500 metres.

## What to see

History is thick on the ground round here. Across the road beneath the trees are the ditches and ramparts of Burfa Camp, an Iron Age hill fort, while the reserve itself embraces the earthworks of a motte and bailey castle. The ravens that croak and buzzards that mew overhead seem to reinforce the sense of timeless continuity.

The 140 recorded flowering plant species mean there is always something of interest to find from the early appearance of bright yellow kingcups, through to the loose pink heads of the appropriately named ragged robin and later the drifts of creamy white meadowsweet. Heath spotted orchids are a speciality of the more acid wet grassland.

The bridges and boardwalks are a necessary improvement for allowing access to the site. The section of walkway after the motte and bailey

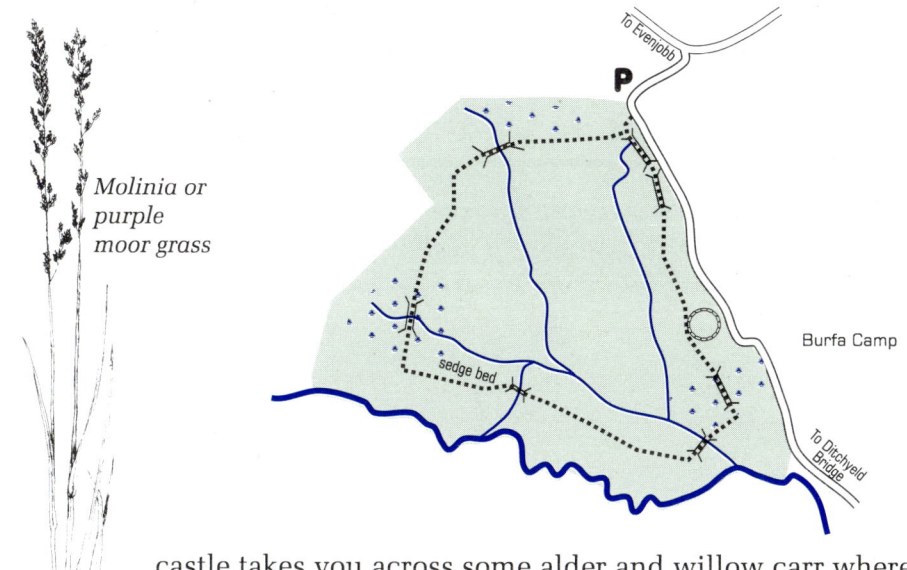

*Molinia or purple moor grass*

castle takes you across some alder and willow carr where active coppicing is being practised, though in contrast there are some enormous alder trees of considerable age.

The trickiest section to cross if the weather has been wet is the sedge bed dominated by sharp sedge, *Carex acutiformis*, which grows in tussocks with very soggy ground between. Posts indicate the approximate direction of the path but there is nothing definite on the ground.

Rising onto the drier pasture in the autumn the grass is full of the yellow waxy looking fungi of the genus *Hygrophorus*.

*Ragged robin*

## Nearby Sites

Apart from the nature reserves there are many other places where you will find ample wildlife in this border country. Offa's Dyke Path follows the Dyke itself here, skirting Burfa Camp across the road from the reserve. Walk it northwards and in barely a mile you come to The Granner, a 20 acre wood owned by the Woodland Trust which makes a most attractive walk. Or get there ½ mile east from Evenjobb. There is room for a few cars to park at the roadside entrance at grid ref. SO 272624.

Arrangements can be made with the Countryside Council for Wales to botanise on the Stanner Rocks NNR by the A44 three miles south of Burfa Bog, where the igneous rocks provide conditions for a variety of very unusual plants.

# 30 ~ Withybeds
## Radnorshire Wildlife Trust

*Three acres of the reserve is a virtual island between the old mill leat and the River Lugg, dominated by a jungle of willow trees. The reserve has been extended recently to include five acres of meadow.*

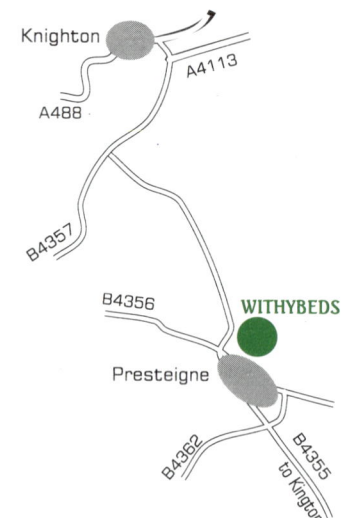

**Maps:** LR 148; PF 971; grid ref: SO 309651.

**Access:** Open at all times. Approached from car park on B4355 or off the public footpath that runs along west edge of the site from Presteigne town centre.

**Parking:** Car park at north end of site off B4355.

**Public Transport:** Infrequent services to Presteigne most days.

**Contact:** RWT on 01597 823298.

**Facilities:** Information boards on site, some with braille; well surfaced path with touching rail runs around the wood. Picnic area.

**Time:** ½ hour on the reserve.

## How to get there

The car park and picnic area is west of Presteigne on the B4355 to Knighton by the river bridge. Or walk from the town down Pound Lane then left on the footpath past the old mill.

## What to see

Despite its small size and close proximity to the town, the Withybeds retain a strong sense of wilderness – jungle even, with a mass of fallen and leaning branches of the large white willow trees. The name of the site would indicate that in the past the willow has been regularly coppiced for "withies", the young flexible stems that were used for willow baskets and similar weaving.

Today the large descendants of these willows dominate the site, and are allowed to grow on uninterrupted as a willow carr (woodland on waterlogged soil). The shaded wet conditions are ideal for other marsh plants including kingcups (marsh marigolds) in the spring and opposite-leaved golden saxifrage. Early summer on the slightly drier ground sees a carpet of the wild garlic or ramsons. Other species to look out for include lady fern, enchanter's nightshade, figwort, water mint and, amongst the trees, small leaved lime.

By contrast five acres of meadowland, called Wentes Meadow after a previous owner, have been added to the reserve between the car park and the wood. This is often grazed to maintain the original management practice which gives it its interesting mix of wildflowers. These include a curious double-flowered form of lady's smock.

Approach the river bank quietly and you might see fish beneath the surface – a largely overlooked group of animals on nature reserves, except by herons and kingfishers that feed on them!

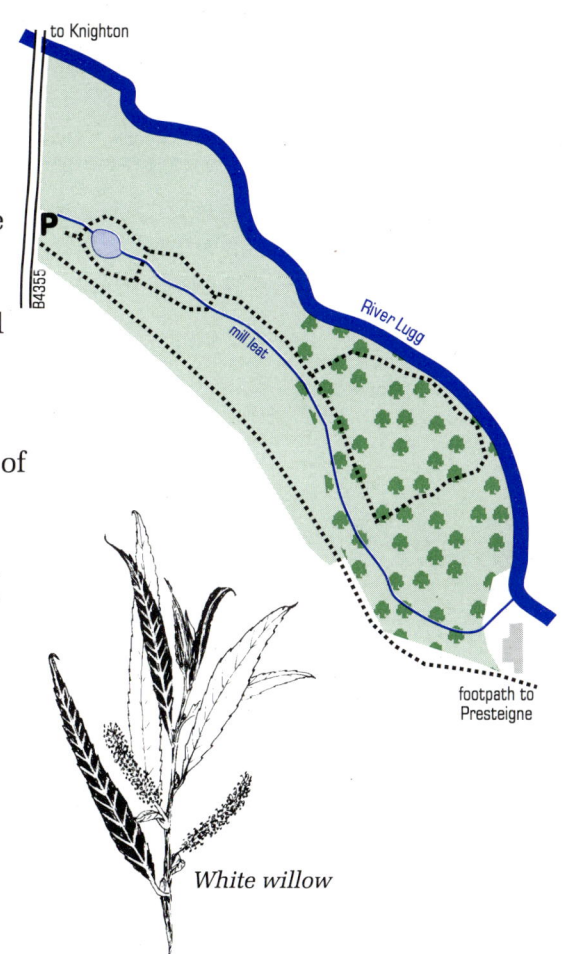

White willow

## Nearby Sites

There is little public access to the River Lugg and its adjacent water meadows, important though they are for wildlife. However, there are opportunities for walking over the hills and through the woods in this delightful border country. The Offa's Dyke National Trail and the Mortimer Trail (Kington to Ludlow) both run close to Presteigne. Guides are available from the Tourist Information Centre.

Silia Wood, ½ mile west of Presteigne (entrance at grid ref. SO 306640) is owned by the Woodland Trust and easily accessible from the town. In the last century it was partly planted up as an arboretum and a number of splendid specimen conifers survive.

# 31 ~ Fron Wood/Garth Dingle
## Woodland Trust

*This reserve of 19 acres is two woods in one: Fron wood has been partly cleared but replanted, while the steep wooded side of Garth Dingle is almost impenetrable. Both have a rich ground flora.*

**Maps:** LR 148 or 161; PF 1015; grid ref: SO 191420.

**Access:** Open at all times via the track and public footpaths that run through the wood.

**Parking:** Usually room up the cul-de-sac by St Meilig's church but avoid service times and have particular regard to not blocking gateways or access.

**Public Transport:** Very sparse bus services on A438.

**Contact:** The Woodland Trust on 01476 581111.

**Facilities:** Clearly marked walk.

**Time:** Allow an hour to stroll around the main circular path through the wood.

## How to get there

Turn west off the A438 on the Painscastle road, opposite the Radnor Arms in the village of Llowes. In a short distance turn right to the church and park neatly so as to obstruct neither the church nor the house entrances. Walk to the wood up the lane which becomes a track through the wood.

## What to see

Garth Dingle is a valley cut deeply into the hillside, which drops steeply away below the path. There is therefore no easy access to this side of the wood, but it does mean you get a good view into the canopy of the oak and ash rooted many feet below.

The ground flora is particularly varied and the wood is one of the richest in the district, earning the status of a Site of Special Scientific Interest (SSSI). On a casual visit it is the commoner plants that impress. Fron Wood was partly cleared a few years ago, before purchase by the Woodland Trust to safeguard it. This is reflected in the spread of bracken in open areas, but it is preceded by a vast sea of bluebells, and replanting should soon restore the

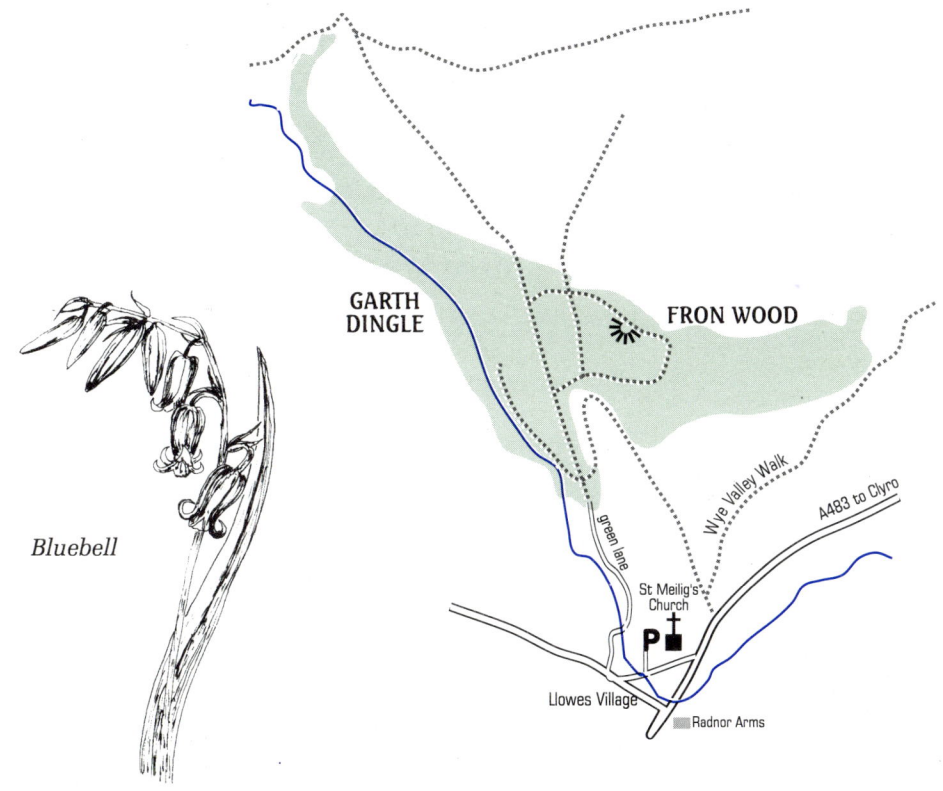

woodland cover. Bluebells should not be taken for granted. Britain is the main stronghold of the bluebell throughout Europe.

At the east end of Fron Wood there survives a substantial stand of hazel and field maple coppice. The latter is a regular but not common native tree of importance for its associated insect fauna, and there are some unusually large specimens to be seen here.

A walk around Fron Wood is rewarded (until the trees grow up!) with splendid views out across the Wye Valley to the Black Mountains.

## Nearby Sites

There is another Woodland Trust wood a mile south west of Garth Dingle, at Cilcenni Dingle. There is an entrance gate at grid ref: 184410, but it is very little visited and access is definitely for the more adventurous.

Fron Wood is another site that is close to the Wye Valley Walk which comes through Llowes, and will lead you on a riverside route from here to Hay-on-Wye. This is Kilvert Country – the autobiographical Rev Kilvert was vicar of neighbouring Clyro and a number of walks are described in locally available leaflets, to places associated with this famous literary cleric.

# 32 ~ Llandeilo Graban

## Radnorshire Wildlife Trust

*This is an unusual nature reserve – the two verges of a stretch of road that was converted from an old railway line. By having a specific management agreement wildlife can be protected.*

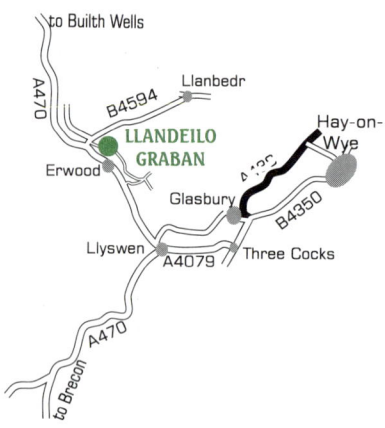

**Maps:** LR 147/148; PF 1015; grid ref: SO 092438 to 105428.

**Access:** Open at all times.

**Parking:** There are laybys along the road, but parking is recommended at the old Erwood station site.

**Public Transport:** Postbus Powys timetable 101. Every few hours on A470, Powys timetable 47.

**Contact:** RWT on 01597 823298.

**Facilities:** Information board at Erwood station as well as picnic tables, refreshments etc.

**Time:** The reserve alone will not occupy you for much more than 1½ hours even if you walk it from Erwood station, but you could easily spend half a day in the vicinity.

## How to get there

Turn north off the A470 on the B4594 (Painscastle and Llanstephan) ¾ mile north of Erwood village, and over the Wye. At T junction turn left then left again to get onto the road that was created from the old Wye Valley railway from Three Cocks to Llanidloes, closed as a railway in 1963 and subsequently made into a road by Powys County Council. The reserve starts where the new road crosses the B4594 and continues for about 1½ miles to the bridge over Ciliau Dingle.

## What to see

The verge was for almost exactly 100 years a trackside strip, enjoying very little interference beyond keeping down the taller growth and almost certainly the occasional fire.

Columbine, woodsage, angelica and common valerian were probably introduced through the use of limestone or basalt railway balast. The bluebells have spread in from adjacent woodland, while the hare's foot clover is a plant of arable fields, relatively rare in Radnorshire.

Most unusual plant of the reserve is Welsh stonecrop, *Sedum fosteranum*,

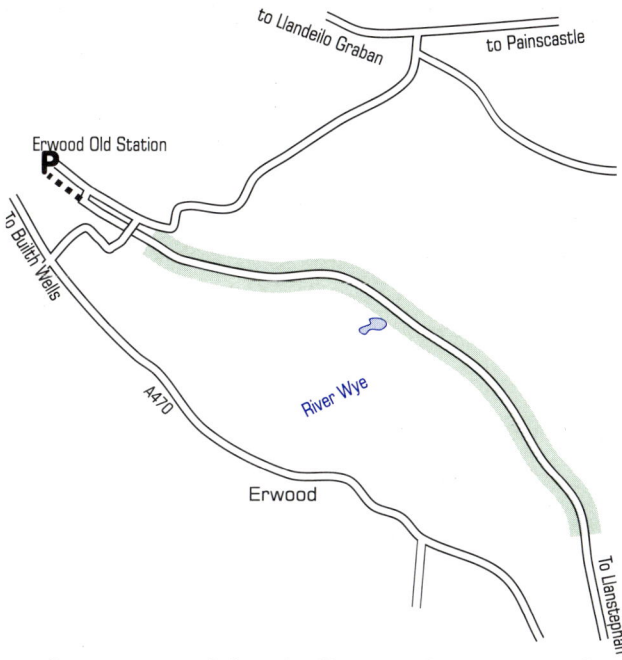

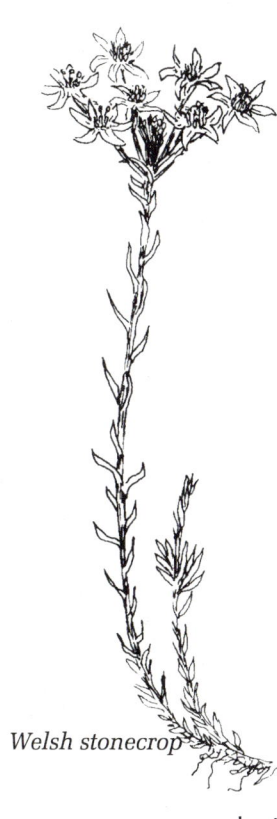
*Welsh stonecrop*

found on some of the shallow rock cuttings of the old line.

The road lets in plenty of light onto the verges, which, like a glade through a wood, harbour a large number of moths and butterflies including small heath, small skipper and dark green fritillary.

There are frequent views out from the road to the south west over parkland with some fine specimen trees and across the flood plain of the River Wye.

---

## Nearby Sites

It must be said that greater general interest attaches to nearby sites than to the reserve itself. You should visit the old Erwood Station; indeed this makes a good parking place and start for a walk down the reserve. The station houses a craft shop and refreshments are available in the summer.

A public footpath leads from a gate opposite the station platform into the wood that clothes this bank of the River Wye. Access is restricted to the path but it is a beautiful wood to wander through with glimpses of the river below.

The road through the reserve is part of the long distance Wye Valley Walk which might tempt you further afield – from the source of the Wye to its mouth at Chepstow!

# 33 ~ Pwllpatti
## Radnorshire Wildlife Trust

*Another unusual reserve for the Radnorshire Wildlife Trust – one you look over, rather than go to; and then mainly in the winter when flood waters attract wildfowl.*

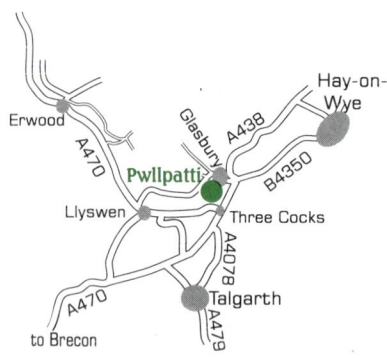

**Maps:** LR 161, PF 1038; grid ref: SO 166393.

**Access:** Hide and viewpoint are available at all times. Please do not go down to the reserve. There is only likely to be anything of interest to see between December and March when the river level rises.

**Parking:** Roadside lay-by.

**Public Transport:** Infrequent service most days. Powys timetables 56 & 53

**Contact:** RWT on 01597 823298.

**Facilities:** Observation hide.

**Time:** Entirely dependent on the interest of the site at the time of your visit. A couple of minutes in passing will ascertain whether birds are there or not.

### How to get there

On the B4350 approached over the river off the A470 at Llyswen, or through Glasbury off the A438. A layby between Pwllpatti Farm and Cwmbach is a few yards north of the observation hide.

### What to see

This site effectively extends the nature watching season into the winter. Indeed in the summer there appears to be little special here: just a pleasant damp hollow in the fields. It marks an ancient meander of the River Wye, now flowing a few hundred metres to the south on the other side of its flood plain. But as water levels rise in the winter the old course of the river is marked by a long shallow pool which attracts wintering wildfowl.

To give a better view of the birds without disturbing them, an observation hide has been built overlooking the site, just within the roadside hedge. Please approach and operate the shutters quietly so as not to frighten the birds you have come to see.

Of special interest are the flocks of swans including the two winter migrants – Bewick's and whooper

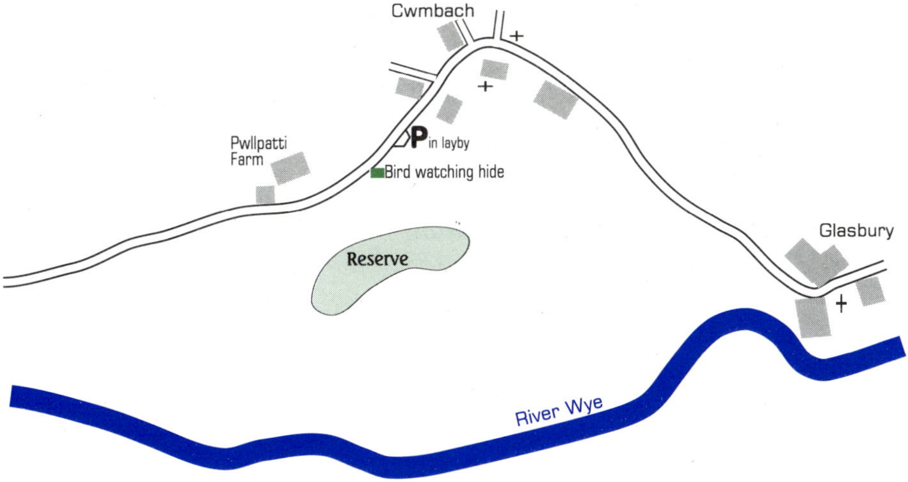

*Whooper swan* 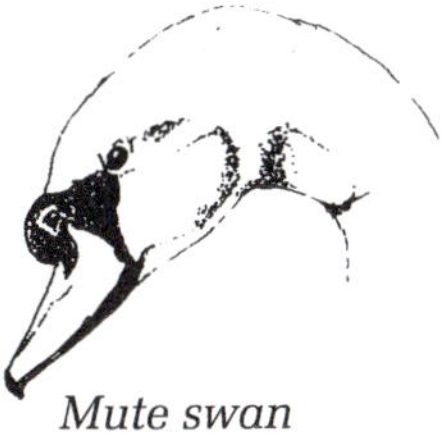  *Mute swan*   *Bewick's swan*

swans. They are distinguished from the mute swan by their black and yellow bills and more upright neck posture, and from each other by the detail of the bill marking. Other wintering birds include wigeon, pochard, gadwall and green sandpiper. If you do call in during the summer the site will be marked by sufficient wetland to support a pair or two of coot, moorhen and mallard. And even if the birds are missing there is a fantastic view across to the northern escarpment of the Black Mountains.

## Nearby Sites

There is a clutch of nature reserves – woodland and wetland – in the vicinity as described on the adjacent pages, so if there is not much happening here, your journey is not wasted.

The Wye Valley Walk will give you a perspective on the area from the other side of the reserve – it runs between the pool and the river, but the other side of the hedge, and is accessible from the road at Glasbury.

Perhaps the view will tempt you across the river at Glasbury and up into the Black Mountains in the footsteps of Francis Kilvert.

# 34 ~ Brechfa Pool
## Brecknock Wildlife Trust

*This 16 acres of common land, with its large shallow pool is just the sort of habitat that could so easily be lost were it not for a sympathetic landowner supporting management for wildlife.*

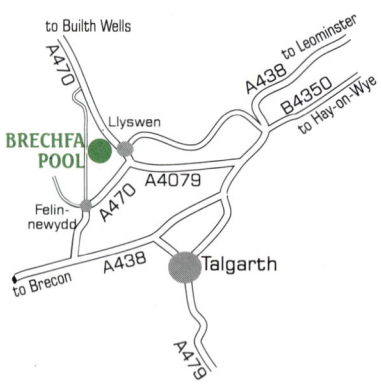

**Maps:** LR 161; PF 1038; grid ref: SO 118377.

**Access:** Open at all times, as unfenced common land, with public bridleway access.

**Parking:** On roadside opposite the chapel.

**Public Transport:** None to site, but only 1½km from bus stop at Llyswen bridge, by extremely steep footpath; Powys timetable 47.

**Contact:** BWT on 01874 625708.

**Facilities:** Leaflet.

**Time:** A quick look in passing will tell you whether there is much to stop for. There is always the view.

## How to get there

Not a place you will go through by chance, but not far from main roads either. The easier route is off the A470 south of Llyswen, steeply up the lane, over the cattle grid and you are on the common with the reserve to your right. The scenic route is off the A470 north of Llyswen at Llangoed (easily missed turning) and winding steeply up through some conifer woodland before levelling out on Brechfa Common.

## What to see

The shallow pool is home to a small colony of breeding black headed gulls, smallest and least sea-dependant of our "sea-gulls"; but only with a black (strictly chocolate brown) head during the breeding season. They may be joined by a few scavenging herring gulls. These are also increasing inland, finding food on rubbish tips.

The vegetation is maintained as close cropped turf by the continued exercising of common rights for grazing sheep and horses. Take care around the pool where the animals have churned up the mud. This possibly favours survival of plants like pillwort and the orange foxtail. The curious "cushions"

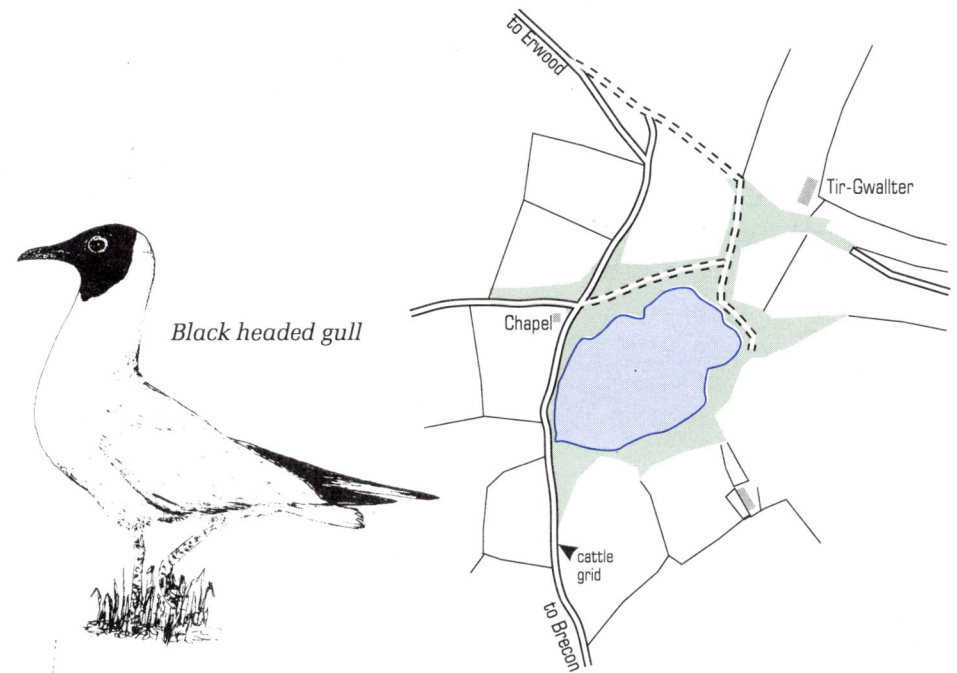

*Black headed gull*

from which the willow trees grow would seem to indicate a higher level in the past, with the tree roots now retaining a ball of soil around them. Indeed the very shallow margins mean that the size of the pool fluctuates considerably with the climate, coming quite close to the road during wet spells.

It may not detain you long, but look in here at any time of year. In winter teal and mallard are usually here. Look also for wigeon, shelduck (with their handsome chestnut collar) and Bewick's swans. At times of spring and autumn migration it is just the sort of pond for waders like redshank, dunlin and black-tailed godwit to drop in on.

The common occupies a plateau perched well up above the surrounding countryside. The views out south-eastwards to the Black Mountain are superb on a good day.

## Nearby Sites

A visit to Brechfa Pool combines well with several other reserves described here such as Pwll y Wrach and Park Wood at Talgarth, or the sites along the River Wye just a few miles away.

Several other areas of open common land survive in the area, including that over Llandefalle Hill at grid ref. SO 070370.

# 35 ~ Park Wood
## The Woodland Trust

*This large and prominent wood of just over 140 acres demonstrates how sensitive management can significantly enhance a wood as both a landscape feature and a habitat for wildlife.*

**Maps:** LR 161; PF 1038; grid ref: SO 167345.

**Access:** Open at all times with a broad more or less level ride through it, but can be wet at times. Extensive silvicultural work is to be done in this wood over the next few years and access to parts may be temporarily restricted.

**Parking:** In the main entrance off the road.

**Public Transport:** Bus to Talgarth from Brecon and Hay, service no. 39.

**Contact:** Woodland Trust on 01476 581111.

**Facilities:** Guide leaflet.

**Time:** Allow at least 1½ hours to wander right through the wood.

## How to get there

From the centre of Talgarth take the lane out of the Square and up past the church. Keep left at the turn to the hospital and on for about a mile to the obvious "bell-mouth" entrance to the wood on the left.

## What to see

The layman will find this wood much more attractive than its ecological description might lead one to expect. As an ex-Forestry Commission plantation of the 1960s it has too many "exotics" for the purist, who might rightly argue that even beech, which was extensively planted, is not strictly native here.

Evidence of its ancient origin is found in the surviving ground flora along the rides and openings, such as yellow archangel. But the beech looks splendid in the spring with its almost translucent green leaves, and tracks through the undergrowth suggest that badger and possibly deer find it attractive enough.

The wood is being selectively thinned to favour the broadleaved element, and re-establishment of oak, ash, rowan and other native species.

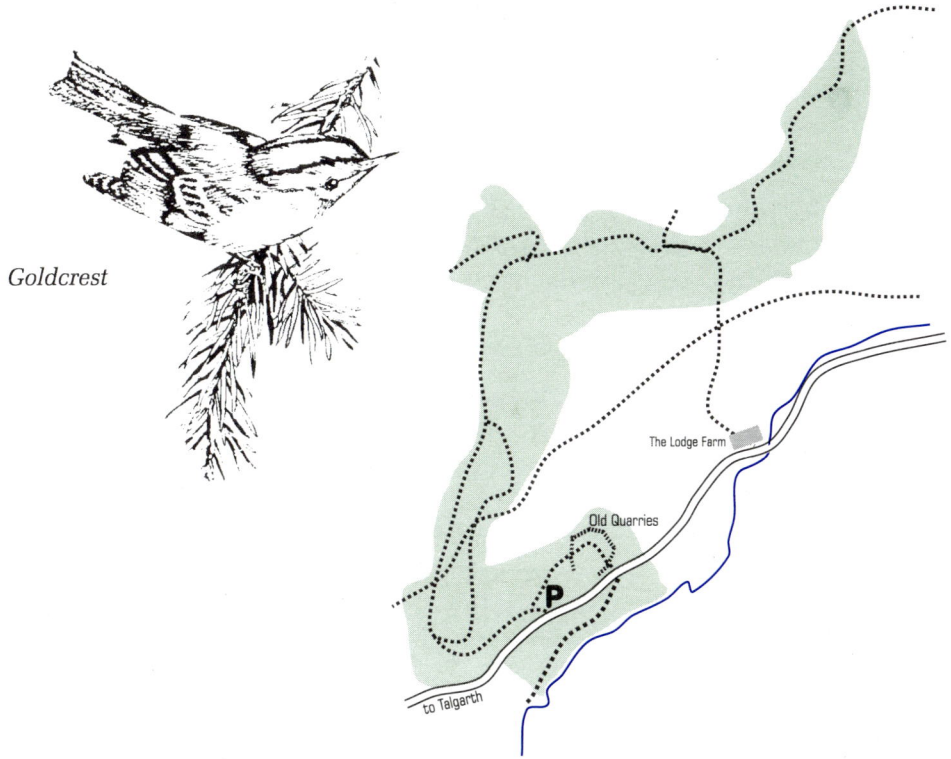

*Goldcrest*

But don't despair of the conifers. Some Douglas fir and western hemlock are being retained to grow into elegantly mature trees and give overall variety to the wood.

Some species of bird, such as the goldcrest and coal tit, positively favour conifer woods. To the specialist the site is of particular interest for its moths, notably three species of *Eriocrania*.

The beech wood to the north of the car park covers the humps and hollows of shallow sandstone quarries. The sandstone here contains thin bands of limestone in which fossil fish and very early plant fossils are sometimes found.

## Nearby Sites

Park Wood contrasts very markedly with Pwll-y-Wrach (see next page). Visit them both while you are here and you will understand the ecologists' preference for the ancient semi-natural oakwood!

Continue up the lane ever more steeply and you pass the archaeological site of two pre-historic long barrows (burial mounds) on your left. Further on, over the cross roads is the upland common of Rhos Fawr. Tracks and bridleways rise steeply up the escarpment to the south east taking you to the fine ridge of the Black Mountains.

# 36 ~ Pwll-y-wrach
## Brecknock Wildlife Trust

*This 21 acre hillside site embodies the essence of all that is best about the wooded dingles of Mid Wales; and everyone can enjoy a visit thanks to the easy access trail through the wood.*

**Maps:** LR 161; PF 1038; grid ref: SO 165326.

**Access:** Public path through the wood, part surfaced as all-ability trail suitable for wheelchairs, pushchairs and partially sighted users. Also permissive paths.

**Parking:** In roadside lay-by at reserve entrance for about 6 cars. Do not obstruct lane or passing places if this is full.

**Public Transport:** Bus to Talgarth on Brecon to Hay service no 39.

**Contact:** BWT on 01874 625708.

**Facilities:** 600m of all-ability trail. Leaflet to reserve and additional geology trail leaflet.

**Time:** Allow at least 1 hour for a complete circuit of the reserve.

## How to get there

From the centre of Talgarth go a short distance south on A479 then take left fork (twice) to Mid-Wales Hospital. Past the hospital the road narrows. Carry on up the lane to the entrance lay-by in 250m. Don't park in other passing places on the lane.

## What to See

This is a splendidly atmospheric wood, with all the wildlife that one associates with the best of this habitat. The surfaced all-ability path descends only very gently through the trees clinging to the valley side, yet because of the lie of the land the path finishes almost at stream level with the wood stretching up to the left. The sure footed can continue along a rougher track to the viewing platform for the waterfall.

Here, likely as not, the dipper will put on a text-book performance running beneath and behind the waterfall in a tireless search for insect larvae.

Flowers are best in the spring and early summer before the shade of the trees gets too heavy. Bluebells carpet the wood. Soils vary widely and the flowers associated with them are distinctive. At the eastern end the soil

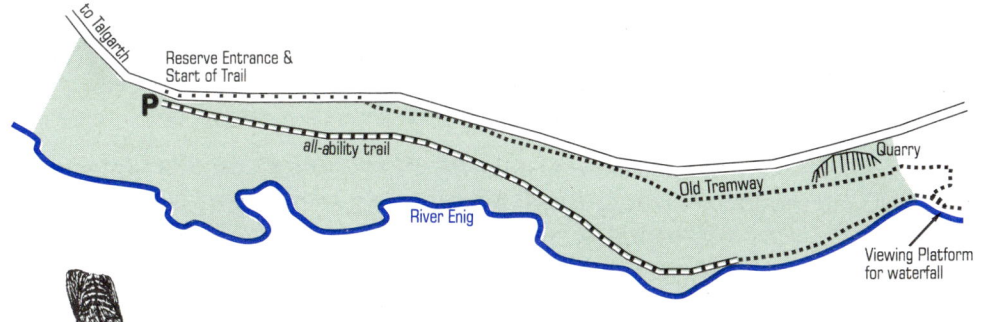

*Dipper*

is richer from the minerals washed out from above. Look out for woodruff early in the year and early purple orchids. Rarities include herb paris, bird's nest orchid and the ghostly looking, leafless toothwort, which lacks its own chlorophyll and lives off the roots of hazel and elm.

The nature of this reserve is determined by the way the stream has cut down into the Old Red Sandstone rock. The thick sequence of predominantly red and purple rocks was laid down about 400 million years ago in huge deltas at the foot of a new mountain chain. Coarse grained sandstone beds alternate with softer silts and mudstones to give the characteristic stepped landscape so clearly seen in the profile of the nearby Black Mountains and Brecon Beacons. The harder steps give rise to waterfalls.

The geological structure is explained more fully on a board by the Pwll y wrach (Witch's Pool) fall. At the top of the wood is a quarry in the sandstone where rock was removed for construction of the Mid Wales Hospital. Examine the structure of the strata here, then follow the old tramway through the wood, onto the lane and back to the start.

Animal life in woods is less conspicuous to the casual visitor. But even if you don't see much on the move, look for clues. This is one of few sites in the region to support a colony of dormice. They eat hazel nuts in a very distinctive way.

## Nearby Sites

There are many nearby nature reserves as listed in the previous and following pages. You are also close to the great sandstone bulk of the Black Mountains. The foot of the escarpment can be reached by continuing up the lane for a further two miles.

Four miles south of Talgarth is Llangorse Lake which accommodates both recreational and natural interests.

# 37 ~ Daudraeth Illtud
## Brecknock Wildlife Trust

*The nature reserve area is 150 acres on the open common land of Mynydd Illtud, the marshy plateau top catchment for the headwaters of streams that feed the Usk.*

## How to get there

Take the minor road SW off the A40 roundabout at the west end of the Brecon by-pass, follow the lane up the spine of the hill to Mynydd Illtyd common and keep going until the second section of unfenced road is reached. Alternatively follow the Brecon Beacons Visitor Centre signs from Libanus on the A470. Keep straight on at the visitor centre turn and left at the T junction.

## What to see

The boggy moorland needs looking at closely if you are to see much in this superficially monotonous habitat; but not too closely in the wetter parts where the ground can be dangerous and there is a real chance of getting stuck.

In the wetter flushes look for the insectivorous duo of sundew and butterwort. A sure sign of acid conditions, low in nutrients, where these two plants supplement their diet with insect protein. Creeping amongst the bogmosses is the low-growing bog pimpernel which puts up its pink trumpet-like flowers at regular intervals off a thin stem. An unusual feature of Traeth Mawr (traeth normally means a

**Maps:** LR 160; PF 1061; grid ref: SN 967256.

**Access:** Open at all times, by paths off the unfenced road across the common. But keep off the very boggy area of Traeth Bach.

**Parking:** Roadside parking, but please do not drive onto the common.

**Public Transport:** About 3km walk from Brecon-Merthyr bus service on A470 at Libanus, Powys timetable 43.

**Contact:** BWT on 01874 625708.

**Facilities:** None.

**Time:** ½ hour will give you time to look over the reserve for interesting arrivals.

*Snipe*

beach or shore but here refers to the boggy heath; mawr = big) is a stand of great fen sedge.

This is curlew, redshank and peewit country, where the distinctive cries of these three birds in particular add so much to the moorland atmosphere. Well camouflaged snipe probe the edges of pools and marshy ground for food, and herons take frogs and insect larvae such as the large and ferocious dragonfly nymphs. Those that survive emerge as the dragonflies that can be seen hawking over the water in summer.

---

## Nearby Sites

The Brecon Beacons National Park Visitor Centre (still often referred to by its old name of the Mountain Centre) is barely a mile away. This will provide you with an introduction to, and all the information you need about, the National Park. You can walk from here to the Daudraeth Illtud reserve along a bridleway shown on the plan above.

The minor road south from the A4215, through the heart of the Brecon Beacons, will bring you in about 8 miles to Ystradfellte, centre for exploration of the famous waterfalls and caves of the Afon Mellte, where walks of varying length are laid out from the car parks.

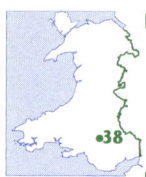

# 38 ~ Craig Cerrig-gleisiad
## Countryside Council for Wales

*This 1200 acre National Nature Reserve is one of the very special places within the Brecon Beacons National Park. The north facing crags towering above the secluded valley harbour many rarities.*

**Maps:** LR 160; PF 1061; grid ref: SN 960220.

**Access:** Open at all times by footpath off the A470.

**Parking:** Lay-by on A470, 5 miles south of Brecon, 1½ miles north of Storey Arms.

**Public Transport:** Bus between Brecon and Merthyr Tydfil, Powys timetable 43.

**Contact:** CCW on 01873 857938.

**Facilities:** Leaflet, information boards, waymarked footpaths.

**Time:** Don't rush it. Come here for half a day and picnic in the area set aside by the road.

## How to get there

The easiest approach is directly from the lay-by on the A40 Brecon to Merthyr Tydfil road about 5 miles from Brecon at grid ref. 972223. A stile takes you over the wall and onto the main path through the reserve.

## What to see

As you go up the path note the singularly appropriate memorial to Eric Bartlett. A wood has been planted in memory of this naturalist who did so much for the National Park and the work of the Brecknock Wildlife Trust.

Look up to the steep north facing crags. You will notice their step-like appearance of alternating hard sandstone bands with softer shaley layers. This reflects the cycles of deposition of sediment when these rocks were forming in a great delta some 400 million years ago.

The carving of the landscape into the shape we see today was brought about by the glaciers of the last Ice Age. Moving ice plucked pieces off the north facing slopes. Many were then dropped by the melting glaciers on the valley floor, or slumped in large landslips, giving rise to the hummocky ground.

*Purple saxifrage*

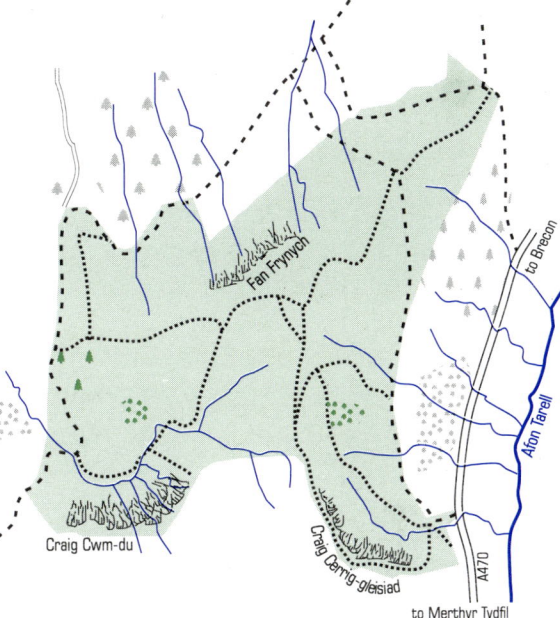

On the bare rocky ledges facing north there survive some of the rare arctic/alpine plants which colonised the landscape as the climate warmed after the Ice Age, and are now generally restricted to more northern latitudes. They can survive here because the sun rarely reaches them and the difficulty of access prevents sheep grazing. Be warned, and follow suit. Do not climb the crags and screes.

There is plenty else to find on this 1200 acre reserve which takes in the summit of Fan Frynych. Over 500 different plants have been recorded as well as 80 species of birds. The aim is to create even more variety by returning native trees to places where they have died out through grazing; and at the same time to manage the open moorland to encourage better heather and bilberry cover.

## Nearby Sites

This is just one of several areas you can explore in the central part of the Brecon Beacons. Two miles down the road towards Merthyr Tydfil is the car park and starting point for walks up to the summit of Pen y Fan.

For the less active there are the reservoirs to be explored alongside the A470, or for moorland views take the A4059 towards Aberdare.

This is also the way through to the valley of the Afon Mellte with its spectacular caves and waterfalls south of the village of Ystradfellte. There is a network of clearly waymarked paths here from the main car park at Gwaun Hepste, where there is a Forest Enterprise visitor centre. It is only a short walk to the main cave of Porth yr Ogof.

North of the reserve 1½ miles off the main road west of Libanus is the Brecon Beacons National Park visitor centre. It has displays on the wildlife and landscape of the park and a shop stocked with local literature, maps and guides.

# 39 ~ Craig y Cilau
## Countryside Council for Wales

*Situated on the high limestone rim of the South Wales coalfield, this spectacular 160 acres of common, crag and wood, has a fascinating history and the wildlife interest of a National Nature Reserve.*

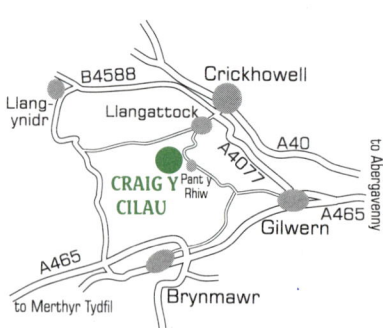

## How to get there

From the A4077 turn south through the centre of Llangattock, fork right at the chapel, over the canal and steeply up the lane for about 1½ miles until you cross onto the unfenced common. Park tidily on the roadside, and head for the crags or take the public footpath first down to the foot of the reserve. Or approach from the east, parking at the old quarrying settlement of Pant-y-rhiw.

**Maps:** LR 161; PF 1080; grid ref: SN 190160.

**Access:** Open at all times via a number of footpaths. Access to Agen Allwedd cave by permit only.

**Parking:** On roadside at edge of common at west end of site, and at Pant y Rhiw to the east.

**Public Transport:** Walk about 3km from bus at Ffawyddog on Brecon-Abergavenny service, Powys timetable 39.

**Contact:** CCW Warden on 01873 857938.

**Facilities:** Leaflet; information boards.

**Time:** There is a good half day's exploration here.

## What to see

The site is of interest to the industrial archaeologist and landscape historian as much as to the naturalist. Quarrying for limestone which comprises the upper part of the cliffs has created a rocky and craggy environment to which the peregrine falcon has now returned to breed.

Above the limestone escarpment is a capping of Millstone Grit and below the limestone are the sandstones, silts and clays of the Old Red Sandstone formation. The reserve therefore enjoys a very wide range of soil types which are reflected in the huge variety of flowering plants.

Clinging to the ledges of the cliffs, out of reach of grazing sheep, there are

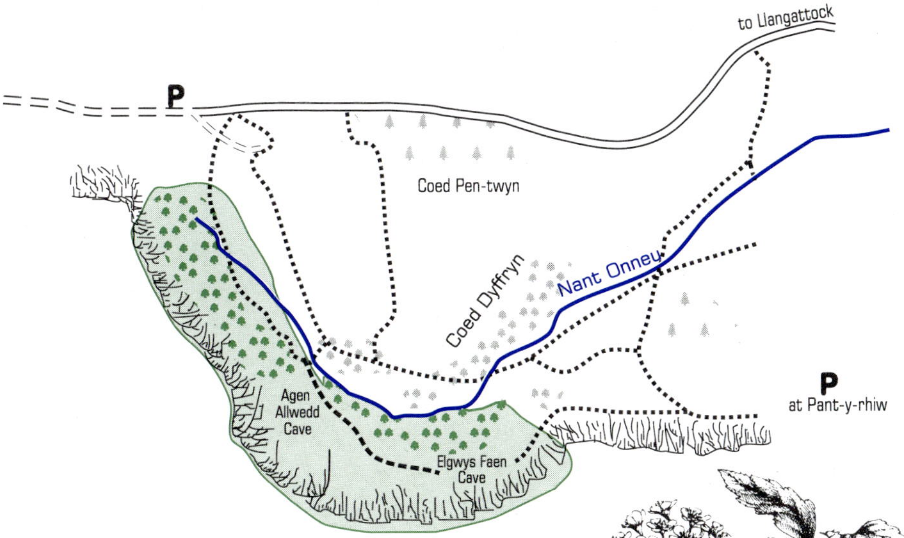

*Whitebeam*

five notable species of whitebeam, one of which is unique to this locality. In the shaded woody area on the lower slopes another rarity in this area is the alpine enchanter's nightshade, here at the southern limit of its distribution in Britain.

The varied habitat from the scrub woodland on the lower slopes, up through the short limestone grassland and sparsely wooded cliffs to the open moorland of the summit makes this an excellent reserve for many different insects and birds. 25 species of butterfly have been recorded.

The cliffs are ideal raven country and the ring ouzel or mountain blackbird returns here each summer along with wood warbler amongst the trees and wheatear on the open land.

The reserve enjoys a further dimension in the extensive cave system which penetrates the limestone.

## Nearby Sites

There is walking available over the common of Mynydd Llangatwg, beyond the limits of the reserve, including a footpath across the summit which drops down to Brynmawr. Here the Nantyglo ironworks was the main consumer of the limestone that was quarried. Other limestone went down tramways to the canal at Llangattock. The limekilns, where the stone was burnt to produce lime for fertiliser, have been restored alongside the canal.

The towpath of the Brecon and Abergavenny Canal makes a pleasant walk as it follows the southern side of the Usk valley.

# 40 ~ Welsh Wildlife Centre
## Dyfed Wildlife Trust

*It is almost back to the coast to end our trail round Mid Wales at a reserve with a difference. Wildlife of wetland, wood and meadow is conserved, while also being made accessible to the public.*

**Maps:** LR 145; PF 1010; grid ref: SN 185455.

**Access:** Open 9.30am to dusk all year. Reserve entrance fee charged. Paths suitable for wheelchairs. Visitor centre 10 - 5, Easter - end Oct. Group booking throughout year.

**Parking:** Car/coach park on reserve.

**Public Transport:** Occasional buses to Cilgerran, service 430.

**Contact:** Centre on 01239 621600 or DWT on 01437 765462.

**Facilities:** All embracing – visitor centre with exhibition, restaurant, craft workshop, animal farm, playground, wheelchair accessible observation hides. Bunkhouse style accommodation on site.

**Time:** This is a place to visit for half a day at least. An ideal day out for the family and introduction to wildlife watching for the children.

## How to get there

Off the A487 2 miles south from Cardigan take the road to Cilgerran. The reserve entrance drive (up the old railway line) is to the north in ½ mile.

## What to see

This reserve is quite unlike any others in this book. Its 260 acres offer both wildlife and visitors an extraordinary range of habitats and facilities respectively.

Primarily it is a wetland nature reserve and SSSI – the second largest reed-bed in Wales, and a stretch of the tidal Afon Teifi on which coracle fishermen still practice their ancient skills. But to the south are broadleaved woods – part of the Coedmor National Nature Reserve – flanking the river gorge and surrounding meadows which preserve the traditional grassland flowers and butterflies.

The reed bed is home to the scarce Cetti's warbler, a bird near the edge of its range here, which has been breeding in Britain only since the 1970s. It flies in each summer with ten other species of warbler including reed, sedge and grasshopper warblers which breed in the reedbeds and wood warbler in the

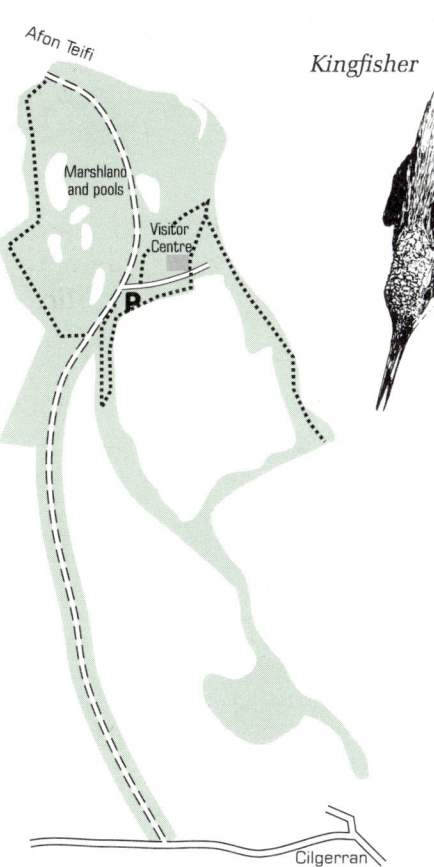

*Kingfisher*

woods. Surprisingly perhaps the reedbeds are also the place to see large numbers of swallows which roost there. The famous 18th century vicar of Selborne, Gilbert White believed swallows hibernated in reedbeds! Certainly they occasionally provide a warmer home for a bittern than its East Anglian nesting grounds.

One of the attractions of the Welsh Wildlife Centre is that there is something to see at all times of the year. In spring and autumn it is a great stopping-off place for migrants, and in the winter the marshes are important for wildfowl.

Access to the wildlife is helped by the five miles of path that thread the site and will take you from the magnificent visitor centre with its full exhibition facilities to any of the hides which may give you a first hand look at otters, red and sika deer or sparrowhawks and ravens. All this on a site which at the turn of the century was a working slate quarry. Today adders and lizards might bask on the quarry floor and bats roost in the old quarry tunnel.

## Nearby Sites

The Cardigan coast between Cardigan and New Quay offers many "wild places" on its rocky cliffs and headlands, as does the valley of the Teifi upstream to Cenarth – another site where you can see coracle fishermen and, in season, watch salmon leaping up the falls.

The Dyfed Wildlife Trust looks after two dozen nature reserves in the area of Mid Wales covered by this book; but before visiting they would prefer that you go first to the Welsh Wildlife Centre or contact Trust Headquarters at Haverfordwest for details and permission.

# Notes

# Notes

# Notes